D1179960

A LEGACY OF
SERVICE

A History of the California Water Service Group

by Kenneth J. Roed

Dedicated to those

who have gone before

Acknowledgments

I t was during the late eighties when I first got the bug to learn more about the history of this great Company, as I became privy to bits and pieces listening to those fine gentlemen, Fred Dodge and Robert Minge Brown, relating wonderful stories of times past. Someday, I thought, I'll write it all down. But retirement came and with it a whole new set of priorities. Gratefully, the call came a few years later from CEO Pete Nelson inviting me to chronicle the fascinating story of California Water Service and of the people who contributed so much to its well-being. So the task began in earnest back in 1999.

The most enjoyable part of journey has been working with so many people who took an interest in the project, offering their time and full support to ensure its success.

Without a doubt the greatest source in helping to bring the past alive has been former Cal Water vice president and chief engineer Jeptha A. Wade, Jr., who started his career some 65 years ago, first as an operations maintenance worker in San Mateo, then as an office boy at the General Office. I am indebted to his wonderful photographic memory, to his hospitality and to his willingness to go above and beyond to help ensure the accuracy of this account. Jep was among scores of retirees, friends of the Company and current employees whom I have recognized in the book's bibliography and to whom I am indebted for their time and interest in relating their own personal experiences in living out the Cal Water story.

So many others have been generously involved in this project including Raymond G. Woolfe, Jr., author of that magnificent book, *Secretariat*; Ciril Wyatt-Donnelly of McCutchen, Doyle, Brown & Enersen; Ray Silvia, Fresno County Library; Julie Holland of J.Holland Design; Phil and Sandy Sims; and Fred Rios, Shannon Dean, Sandy Dean, Yvonne Hung, San Thompson and Karen Lichtenberg of Cal Water. I thank all for the expertise each has lent to this endeavor.

Kenneth J. Roed

Prologue

The history of the California Water Service Group and its subsidiary, Cal Water, is a fascinating tale largely because of the people who have made the Company what it is today. A Legacy of Service debunks a commonly held view that life in a utility is uneventful or even dull at times. From thoroughbred horse racing to Sgt. Juan Jose Dominguez and the Spanish land grants, there's something in this story for everyone who likes a good yarn.

For those of us who today are living and creating present day history, reviewing our past can also be a sobering experience. It's almost like hearing voices calling out, "Hey, take good care of this Company. It took our sweat and tears to make it what it is today."

We're no longer just Cal Water, but a group of companies that now includes Washington Water, New Mexico Water, Hawaii Water and CWS Utility Services. However, we have all grown from the same seed that took root back in 1926.

In the past 78 years, we have built a reputation for being a leader in providing innovative and traditional utility services to our customers and our communities. Doing so took the dedication of our employees, who overcame adversities, embraced change and made the most of opportunities that came our way. With deep gratitude and pride, we salute all employees, past and present, for making it happen.

Robert W. Foy
Chairman of the Board

Peter C. Nelson
President and Chief Executive Officer

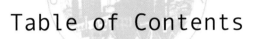

Table of Contents

Chapter	Page

Chapter 1

"This is Mr. Rockefeller calling..."

Ralph Elsman never forgot the day he made his first executive decision. The year was 1905, and the 20-year-old utility worker, who would one day take the helm of California Water Service Company, had just won a great promotion. He had been assigned the task of running the electric generator plant for the Westchester Lighting Company.

While on duty at the Brooklyn-based firm, Elsman answered the phone to a booming voice on the other end.

"This is Mr. Rockefeller calling. I wonder if you could come out and talk to me. I have a matter I wish to discuss with the lighting company."

For even the self-assured Elsman, receiving a call from one of his suburban utility customers who just happened to be the world's richest man, was, to say the least, an unsettling moment.

As requested, Elsman arrived for a 6 a.m. appointment the following day and was greeted cordially by Rockefeller, who proceeded to make an unusual request: *"All right, son, please take your shoes and socks off. I'd like to give you a tour of my gardens."*

For the next hour, the two barefooted men strolled through acres of beautifully manicured, dew-laden grass before finally, Rockefeller ushered his guest into his home.

"Now, what I want to see you about," Rockefeller began. *"Mrs. Rockefeller suffers from the heat something awful, and she has this new device that has been invented called the electric fan and it really helps to cool her. The only trouble is there isn't any electricity in the*

daytime when it's hot. Do you suppose you could arrange to turn the generators on just a bit earlier during the day so she can run the fan and keep cool?"

It was an unusual request, but as Elsman would later recall, he did not hesitate a single moment before making the first executive decision of his long utility career. *"Yes, Mr. Rockefeller, we certainly can do that."*

So to accommodate his prominent customer, Elsman began to run the plant generators during the daytime, a procedure that, heretofore, had been limited to the evening hours. Electrical power had been used primarily for lighting in those days.

A month passed before Elsman received a call from Mr. Mellon of the Mellon Bank, who had more than a passing interest in the financial well-being of the lighting company. *"What is this I hear about you driving up expenses by running the generators during the daytime?"* Mellon demanded. Elsman proceeded to tell the banker about Rockefeller's call and of his special request. There was a long pause as Mellon digested Elsman's explanation before bellowing, *"Well, I'm glad someone in this outfit has some sense."*

Many years later, Ralph Elsman would be making his most dramatic decisions on behalf of California Water Service Company as he served as chief executive throughout two of the Company's most perilous decades. And once again the name Mellon would surface in support of his efforts.

During this period shortly after the turn of the century, an Elsman contemporary, Christopher T. Chenery, was charting the course of his own career, one that would eventually lead to his founding of California Water Service Company. The paths of the two executives would cross in 1939 when Company ownership changed and Ralph Elsman assumed command from its founder and chief executive.

Christopher T. Chenery
Company Founder

*Chief executive of the Company until 1939 when
Cal Water was sold to General Water, Gas and Electric
Company. An avid horseman and breeder of
thoroughbred race horses, Chenery was also president
of Federal Water Service Company, the parent
of California Water Service.*

Chapter 2

Horse of the Century...

Christopher T. Chenery created California Water Service Company in the fall of 1926 along with two associates, Thomas Hollis Wiggin, a renowned consulting engineer, and George Lewis Ohrstrom, a New York investment banker. The California company, to become known over time as "Cal Water," would be part of Chenery's growing network of operating water utilities that fell under control of his Federal Water Service Company, a New York-based holding company.

Although Chenery was a well-known figure in the public utilities industry, he became more prominently recognized in the world of thoroughbred horse racing. Approximately ten years after his founding of California Water Service Company, Chenery would seriously embrace the racing sport as an owner and breeder.

He reportedly recounted how he began by buying *"four or five horses for a moderate price and a good 16-year-old named Whiskaway for $115."* He would say that the purchase price does not always represent what a horse is worth, but rather *"only what some fool thinks he's worth."* But time would prove that Chenery, a self-made man, was no fool, especially when it came to thoroughbred horse racing. Among his very first purchases was a yearling filly named Hilderes, which cost him $750. Chenery would realize earnings of more than $3 million from Hilderes' offspring line even though the filly herself never raced. He believed that the quality of his mares would be the key to successful breeding.

While New York City was the base for his utility operations, his Meadow Stable in Doswell, Virginia, 20 miles north of Richmond, served as headquarters for his horse racing and breeding activities. From 1939 through 1972, he reportedly earned more than $8.5 million in racing purses and another $12 million in breeding sales. However, despite his early successes in racing, he did not achieve his goal of winning a Kentucky Derby until the latter part of his life. When Meadow Stable did capture its first Derby with the thoroughbred Riva Ridge in 1972, Chenery, now in declining health at age 85, was too ill to attend the race. He reportedly watched it on television from his hospital bed. By this time, his daughter, Penny Chenery Tweedy, had taken over the operations of his racing and breeding enterprise.

Another fast-rising star of Chenery's Meadow Stable was named Horse of the Year for 1972. The magnificent performance of that thoroughbred the following year would bring it the unofficial title of "Horse of the Century." But the Triple Crown victories of Meadow Stable's famed Secretariat during the 1973 season would come too late for Cal Water's founder and legendary utility executive. Chenery died on Jan. 3, 1973, several months prior to Secretariat's spectacular victories in the Kentucky Derby, the Preakness and the Belmont Stakes.

Prior to Secretariat's dramatic Triple Crown performances, Chenery's daughter, Mrs. Tweedy, reportedly faced heavy taxes that burdened her father's estate. To meet this obligation, she agreed to syndicate her famous horse for breeding, selling 32 shares at $190,000 a piece.

In January of 1973, several weeks after her father's death, Mrs. Tweedy paid him high tribute before a throng of 1,100 guests from the world of thoroughbred racing. They had gathered at the Century Plaza Hotel in Los Angeles for the annual Eclipse Awards ceremonies honoring trainers, owners and breeders who had excelled in their profession. Chenery's Meadow Stable was being honored that evening as racing's leading owner, leading breeder and winner of the title "Horse of the Year" for its magnificent thoroughbred, Secretariat.

"Dad had set the standards," Mrs. Tweedy told the banquet gathering, *"and they were high ones."*

Nearly a half century earlier, Christopher T. Chenery had set the standard of quality for his new West Coast utility, California Water Service Company, and it too was high. It was a standard that demanded the very best in personnel and operating systems to ensure its success.

Chapter 3

Cal Water's founding team...

With a zest for life probably unique among most men, Chenery has been described as "a bold, energetic man who loved to ride the wild places." An avid polo player and fox hunter, he reportedly rode daily until his health declined in his sixties. He almost always rode his thoroughbreds.*

Born in Richmond, Virginia, on Sept. 18, 1886, the son of James and Ida Chenery, he spent his boyhood years in Virginia, later enrolling at Washington and Lee University where he studied engineering and was elected to the scholastic society, Phi Beta Kappa. After graduation, he was employed as an engineer on projects in Oregon, Washington and Alaska, where he reportedly participated in the building of a 500-mile railroad.

During World War I, he served as a major in the Army Corps of Engineers, commanding training facilities at Camp Humphries, Virginia. It was during this time he developed a close working relationship with Lt. Col. Thomas H. Wiggin, his commanding officer. Nearly a decade later, Wiggin would become his associate in the founding of Federal Water Service Company of New York and its subsidiary, California Water Service Company.

Persuading Wiggin to become involved in his water company ventures was an astute move by Chenery. Wiggin was well on his way to becoming recognized as a nationally-known civil engineer

*Secretariat *by Raymond G. Woolfe, Jr.*

who was a consultant to more than 100 water companies. He brought prestige and credibility to Chenery's growing utility network, being assigned the task of overseeing engineering for all Federal Water Service's operating utilities, including its West Coast subsidiary, California Water Service Company. An 1895 graduate of the Massachusetts Institute of Technology, Wiggin had been named chairman of an important committee advising the New York City Board of Water Supply, serving as a consultant on the design of the City's public water system. Builders of a major flood control project in China had also called upon him to assist in its development.

The third founding member of the Chenery team that created California Water Service Company was also a veteran of World War I. George Lewis Ohrstrom had served as an Army fighter pilot during the war and was credited with shooting down the last German aircraft as the conflict neared its end during the fall of 1918. Ohrstrom's expertise in stock and bond transactions and investment banking helped generate the capital for Chenery's utility enterprises. In 1919, Ohrstrom had become an investment banker with R. W. Chapman Company of New York City after graduating from the University of Michigan. In 1926, he resigned his position with the firm as vice president in charge of its New York office to form his own organization, G. L. Ohrstrom & Co. It was the same year he joined forces with Chenery and Wiggin to form both the Federal Water Service Company and its subsidiary, California Water Service Company. There was no doubt Ohrstrom was well connected within the business and financial community. In addition to serving as a director of Federal Water Service, Ohrstrom had been elected to the board of directors of 11 other companies, some still familiar today, such as Dresser Manufacturing Company and Prentice Hall Inc.*

With Wiggin providing the engineering stature and experience and Ohrstrom affording his reputation and skills within the investment community, Chenery's entrepreneurial expertise and endeavors were well-complemented.

*Others included Oklahoma Gas Corp., National Gas Corp., Peoples Light and Power Co., Associated Securities Investors, Westvaco Corp., Tri-Utilities Corp., Power, Gas and Water Securities Corp., Starrett Corp. and Eastern Exchange Bank .

Chapter 4

The roar of the Twenties...

During the mid-1920s, when Chenery began his acquisition efforts to build a water utility base in California, the nation was experiencing one of its greatest economic booms.

Fueling the dramatic growth of the "Roaring Twenties" was the fast-moving pace of industrialization, technological advancements and the billions of dollars being invested in a spiraling stock market. Amid this prosperity, entrepreneurs recognized the potential that lay in offering the public an opportunity to invest in the booming utilities industry. The stock market provided the vehicle for capitalizing on the nation's insatiable desire for potential gains through securities speculation.

Chenery's Federal Water Service Company, along with numerous utility holding companies, was established for the purpose of acquiring operating companies as subsidiaries. Each subsidiary would provide the holding companies a marketing vehicle for promoting public stock sales. Abuses in stock market activity occurred in many areas throughout the utility industry with no regulatory controls effectively in place.

The federal government's efforts to stamp out such abuses eventually resulted in the passage of the Public Utility Holding Company Act of 1935 (PUHCA). Publicly held utility holding companies would come under regulation by the newly established Securities and Exchange Commission. This legislation and its implications for Chenery's Federal Water Service Company and its subsidiary, California Water Service Company, will be discussed in a later chapter.

When Chenery entered the California market in 1926, he depended heavily upon his locally appointed representatives to ensure the success of his new water company, while he personally operated almost solely from his New York headquarters of Federal Water Service Company. Retaining one of San Francisco's leading law firms was the first order of business when Chenery began his search for water utility properties in the Golden State. He sought a firm that not only provided him the very best in legal representation, but also, through association, brought stature and reputation to his new company.

His choice to be his official "on the scene" corporate and legal counsel was McCutchen, Olney, Mannon and Greene, recognized as one of the City of San Francisco's most reputable firms. He had also based his selection upon McCutchen's background in California water law and its impressive client list, which included the Spring Valley Water Company. Spring Valley was a private water utility serving the City of San Francisco despite the City's ongoing campaign to acquire the system for municipal operation.

Attorneys of the San Francisco firm would be responsible for overseeing the formation of Chenery's new subsidiary as a California corporation. Edward J. McCutchen, senior partner of the law firm, was a native Californian from San Jose and son of survivors of the tragic Donner Party that had crossed the Sierra in 1847. He was a respected San Francisco jurist who was described as "unquestionably the most visible local lawyer of his time."* This type of stature in his local agents was most important to Chenery as he sought to gain prominence for his new California company. In memorializing Mr. McCutchen years later, his associate at the law firm, A. Crawford Greene, Sr., characterized him as a man *"with the strongest of moral*

*David Balabanian, chair of McCutchen, Doyle, Brown, 1995-1999

and ethical principles, of enormous industry with astonishing intuition, all with an overall personal magnetism which drew associates, clients and judges to him." Mr. McCutchen's firm was a perfect fit for Chenery. In ensuing years, the law firm would represent the water company on matters before the State's utility regulators. Its partners would play an important ongoing role in the development and success of California Water Service Company.

From the very beginning, McCutchen attorneys served among Chenery's interim directors with two of the firm's senior partners, A. Crawford Greene, Sr. and Warren Olney, Jr., later named to the permanent board of directors. Greene would serve on the Cal Water Board for almost four decades. Another long-time McCutchen attorney, Robert Minge Brown, would become Cal Water's chairman and chief executive in 1961. He had joined McCutchen in 1934, becoming a senior partner after World War II. His name was included in the firm's title when it evolved into McCutchen, Doyle, Brown & Enersen in 1958.

To assist in his selection of operating water systems in California, Chenery reached out to another San Francisco company, Loveland Engineering. The firm had worked previously for the California Railroad Commission in conducting valuation studies of private water utility systems. The Railroad Commission had been established in 1911 by a state constitutional amendment and its duties were clarified and expanded with the Public Utilities Act of 1912. The Commission's regulatory authority covered railroads, marine transportation companies and utilities, including private water companies. In 1946, it was renamed the California Public Utilities Commission (CPUC). The engineering valuation studies provided by the Loveland firm were important for the Commission's regulatory tasks. They were also important to Chenery in determining the value and condition of those operating water systems he would seek to acquire for Federal Water Service Company.

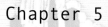

Chapter 5

Let the acquisitions begin...

Chenery established his foothold on the West Coast in four California communities during the fall of 1926 through the acquisition of five separate water systems:

Chico Water Supply Co. .... Oct. 14, 1926
Visalia City Water Co. .... Oct. 15, 1926
Bakersfield Water Works .... Oct. 15, 1926
Electric Water Co. (Bakersfield). .... Oct. 15, 1926
Fresno City Water Co. .... Oct. 18, 1926

He acquired two more systems the following month:

Chico-Vecino Water Co. .... Nov. 6, 1926
W. E. White Water Co. (Chico) .... Nov. 15, 1926

As 1926 came to an end, these seven water systems created the nucleus of California Water Service Company in four operating districts: Chico, Visalia, Bakersfield and Fresno. The Company would be incorporated in the State of California on Dec. 21, 1926, with all stock held by Chenery's Federal Water Service Company of New York. Following the incorporation, the McCutchen law offices on the 13th floor of the Balfour Building at 351 California Street, served as Chenery's temporary San Francisco headquarters for legal and corporate matters. The attorneys also filled in as Chenery's interim directors. At the first meeting of the Board of Directors on Dec. 21, 1926, J. M. Mannon, Jr. of the McCutchen firm, was elected the interim president, and interim directors were Robert L. Lipman, Henry D.

Costigan, Edwin S. Pillsbury, William E. Wright, John G. Eliot and John G. Baldwin.

The first General Office for Company operations was located in Fresno, California, in the San Joaquin Light and Power Building, which today is a landmark office building in the downtown area. As Federal Water Service Company took control of each operating water company, it retained all the managers and employees because the holding company itself did not have the personnel to operate the new acquisitions.

The staff from the Fresno City Water Company, which had been owned by Pacific Gas & Electric Co., would comprise the statewide leadership for Chenery's new Company, providing him with a gold mine in executive talent. The ready-made management team would prove to be a most valuable asset to the new Company for both the short and long term. C. B. "Charlie" Jackson, who was superintendent of the Fresno water system, was named Cal Water's vice president and general manager in charge of statewide operations. Among the other Fresno personnel joining the new Company were Laurence L. Camy, H. K. "Bucky" Harris, Jr., E. K. "Kirby" Barnum, Harlan E. Hulick, Ralph E. Shupe, Frank Suters and E. B. Walthall. Barnum was named a Cal Water vice president and the Company's first chief engineer, with Harris serving as his assistant and later as chief engineer during the 1940s.

Camy, who had been a timekeeper for the Fresno City Water Company, eventually became manager for Cal Water's East Los Angeles District in 1935 and rose to become general manager for the entire Company during the 1950s. A Camy family member has been affiliated with the Company during every year of its 78 years of operation. Laurence Camy's son, Mike, served the Company for more than 37 years before retiring in March of 2001 as district manager in Stockton; and Mike's son, Doug, is a utility worker in the Visalia

District. Laurence Camy's brother, Al, was a superintendent in the Bakersfield District during the 1940s.

Hulick, at age 19, was initially assigned as clerk in the Bakersfield District, but he eventually rose through the ranks to become a Company vice president and treasurer before his untimely death in 1958 at age 50. Shupe, during his 40-year career with Cal Water, became assistant secretary, assistant treasurer and Company controller. Suters became chief accountant for the new Company, and during his subsequent years with Cal Water, would also serve as manager of districts in San Mateo, Chico, Hermosa-Redondo and Stockton.

But of all the Fresno alumni, perhaps the most dramatic story belongs to E. B. Walthall. A bookkeeper and bank teller during his early career, he had worked more than 20 years for the San Joaquin Light and Power Company in Fresno, which had also owned the Fresno City Water Company. Walthall had been assistant general manager of the San Joaquin company at the time it was acquired by PG&E. When PG&E sold its Fresno water properties to Chenery and his Federal Water Service Company, Walthall made the decision to join the new Cal Water team. It was a choice he would not regret. Chenery immediately recognized the talents Walthall brought to his new operations and appointed him Cal Water's first secretary-treasurer and named him to the Company's first permanent Board of Directors. Walthall advanced to vice president in 1928. For a period of 14 years, Walthall assisted Chenery in the acquisitions and mergers of almost all the utility properties that would comprise California Water Service Company.

While he was putting his California executive team in place, Chenery began to set his sights on additional water properties in the Northwest, forming Federal Water's second West Coast subsidiary, the Oregon-Washington Water Service Company. In 1926, he purchased operating water systems in the Washington communities of Vancouver, Hoaquim, and the Skagit Valley towns of Mt. Vernon, Burlington and Sedro Woolley, while in Oregon, he acquired the water system in Salem, the state capital. Chenery retained all employees of the Northwest acquisitions and initially provided management support from personnel operating at the California headquarters.

Chenery's California acquisitions accelerated during the first four months of 1927. On January 26, he purchased two systems — the Port Costa Water Company in northern California's Contra Costa County, with service to Port Costa, Crockett and nearby Valona, and the Hermosa-Redondo Water Company in Los Angeles County. These acquisitions were followed by the purchase of six municipal water systems owned by PG&E for the sum of $2,509,875. They served the communities of Livermore, Stockton, Willows, Dixon, Oroville and Redding. From April 19 through April 26, Chenery merged his total 15 statewide operating systems into one official entity, California Water Service Company.

Prior to this time, the properties had been held in the name of C. B. Jackson, who had served as Chenery's nominee on behalf of Federal Water Service, their legal owner. By having Jackson representing his interests in the California acquisitions, Chenery sought to lessen any possible concerns a community might have regarding ownership of the local water system by out-of-state interests. In its decision on March 21, 1927, the California Railroad Commission authorized the purchase and transfer of the 15 operating water systems from C. B. Jackson (Federal's nominee) to California Water Service Company. The purchase price of the properties was not to exceed $9,422,475. The Railroad Commission also granted California Water Service Company permission to *"issue and sell $2,000,000 of common stock and such additional common preferred stock and bonds* *as may hereafter be authorized, not to exceed $9,422,475."*

With the merger of his California systems now complete and approval from the Railroad Commission in hand, Chenery would form his permanent Board of Directors. At the April 28, 1927, Board meeting, he accepted the resignations of his interim directors who had served since the incorporation on Dec. 21, 1926. Chenery was elected president and a member of the Board along with the following new directors: E. B. Walthall, E.K. Barnum, Russell Lowry and Warren Olney, Jr. Remaining as directors were C. B. Jackson and A. Crawford Greene from the original Board. Greene and Olney were attorneys from the McCutchen law firm, which would continue as the Company's "principal place of business" until December 1927, when the Company established its own San Francisco office space in Room 412 of the Hunter-Dulin Building at 111 Sutter St. The following month, on Jan. 30, 1928, the office would relocate to the building's 10th floor in Room 1029. The Hunter-Dulin Building, today known as 111 Sutter St., was one of the City's premier downtown office locations, and it was where C. B. Jackson, E.B. Walthall and E. K. Barnum organized the Company's executive staff. Operational activities continued to be based in Fresno, while Chenery conducted business from his Federal Water Service offices in New York City.

As 1927 came to a close, the Company's first official totals listed 50,735 customers served within 12 California communities through 15 operating water systems. The annual report for the year covered a period from April 19 to Dec. 31, 1927, combining the financial summaries for Federal Water's two West Coast subsidiaries, California Water Service Company and Oregon-Washington Water Service Company. Gross revenue was $1,370,773. Plant and property were valued at $15,515,845.

Several more water systems in California had been acquired

by Federal Water in 1927. However, four of the new utilities would not be merged into California Water Service until March 31, 1928, including water systems in Petaluma, Stockton, and unincorporated sections of Los Angeles County known as East Los Angeles and Montebello.

Two of the acquisitions — Hanford, located in the San Joaquin Valley, acquired in December 1927, and Bay Point Utilities Co., serving Port Chicago and Concord, acquired in January 1928 — would not merge into California Water Service until Jan. 1, 1929. On Nov. 22 of that year, Federal purchased the Marysville Water Company, merging the system into California Water Service on Feb. 28, 1930.

Federal's acquisition of the Belvedere Water Corporation in East Los Angeles is especially noteworthy because of its future impact on the California company. The Belvedere system became the nucleus of the East Los Angeles District, and the Belvedere manager, Fred L. Dodge, would begin a 57-year career with California Water Service Company. His service included ten years as Company president.

Charles Benton Jackson (C.B. Jackson)
Superintendent of Fresno City Water, he was named vice president and first head of Cal Water's statewide operations.

The Fresno Alumni...

Among the very first water systems making up the Cal Water network in 1926 was the Fresno City Water Company which had been owned by Pacific Gas & Electric Co. Joining the Cal Water team were eight outstanding Fresno City employees whose abilities would shine throughout their careers with the new Company. Not shown here but among the eight was E. K."Kirby" Barnum, who became a Cal Water vice president and its first chief engineer. He appears in a group photograph on page 41.

Harlan E. Hulick
Joining Cal Water at age 19, he would rise to become Company vice president and treasurer.

Laurence L. Camy
Served as district manager in East Los Angeles and later became a Company officer and general manager of statewide operations.

E.B. Walthall
He retired from the Company as vice president in 1940 and as a member of the Board of Directors in 1952.

H.A. "Bucky" Harris Jr.
His 27-year Company career included service as chief engineer from 1944 to 1952.

Ralph H. Shupe
His 40-year Cal Water career would include service as assistant secretary, assistant treasurer and controller.

Frank Suters
He served as chief accountant and district manager in San Mateo, Chico, Hermosa-Redondo and Stockton.

In this mid-1920s scene, personnel of the Visalia City Water Company are shown outside the commercial office at 116 South Church St. The Visalia system was among Cal Water's first statewide acquisitions purchased in October of 1926. Shown from left are Catarino Pizarro, Alfred Winfield, Bill Maskel, Ola Whitt Doughtery, Mr. Davis and Bertha Hass King.

The Redding District and its staff became part of the Cal Water network in 1927, one of six Northern California water systems purchased that year from PG&E.

27

Copy of the original check in the amount of $9,422,475 dated April 25, 1927, signed by Cal Water's C. B. Jackson and E. B. Walthall, enabling the Company's purchase of its first water systems in Chico, Port Costa, Fresno, Visalia, Bakersfield, Hermosa-Redondo, Stockton, Oroville, Redding, Willows, Dixon and Livermore. The systems had originally been purchased by Federal Water Service, Cal Water's New York holding company, with Jackson serving as Federal's nominee in the transactions.

When Cal Water purchased the Fresno City Water Company in 1926, it conducted statewide operations from Room 401 in the San Joaquin Power Building in downtown Fresno. The structure today serves as an office building and community landmark.

Chapter 6

"Please do not think we are boasting..."

In the midst of his early buying spree, Chenery had also set his sights on acquiring the San Jose Water Works. As 1928 came to a close, from his New York office he telephoned senior Cal Water executive C.B. Jackson in San Francisco, directing him to make an initial contact with San Jose Water Works and offer to purchase all of the Company's stock at $125 per share. Even in those days, the San Jose company was considered one of the state's premier private water utilities. On December 18, 1928, Jackson telegrammed Chenery in New York:

> *"Mr. Chenery...*
>
> *Following your telephone communication, I approached*
> *Mr. Kittredge, manager of the San Jose Water Works,*
> *stating I felt our company would be willing to offer $125*
> *for all the stock. We have learned since, that offer will be*
> *well received. Can we make a firm offer on behalf of Federal?*
> *Jackson"*

But Chenery's hopes of acquiring San Jose Water Works were dashed in October of 1929 when General Water, Gas and Electric Company announced it had purchased controlling interest in the San Jose company for $5.1 million, a few days following the stock market crash on October 24.

Jackson had been a fervent advocate of Cal Water and of the importance of private ownership of utilities. He left little doubt about his enthusiasm and loyalty to his California company. Interviewed by the *Magazine of Western Finance* in September of 1928, Jackson commented:

"Please do not think we are boasting, but I may aver that the California Water Service Company has many times proved its worth and usefulness to these communities by more efficient operation and a higher class of service to its many patrons."

By this time in 1928, Cal Water was operating 22 water systems in California from Chico in the north to Los Angeles in the south. Jackson would agree that *"public utilities were, at the time, subjected to keen scrutiny, criticism and even suspicion, supporting the view that propaganda has made for this unwarranted prejudice and adverse feeling."*

An outspoken advocate of private ownership, Jackson would maintain, *"We are daily proving the advantages held by public service corporations, privately owned, over municipally controlled systems."* He delighted in quoting President Coolidge, who contended that *"municipal ownership of public utilities is fundamentally an economic fallacy because the consumer becomes at once the owner and user...the employer and worker...a well-nigh physical impossibility."*

As the decade neared its end, Chenery was preparing to send his own team out from New York to take over the leadership of the California company. Earl C. Elliott, who had been serving as vice president of Federal Water Service Company in New York, was named president of Cal Water in May of 1929. The transition in leadership ended C. B. Jackson's direct role in upper management for California Water Service Company, although he was given new responsibilities as head of Federal's subsidiary operations in Oregon and Washington and later as manager of the Company's San Francisco Peninsula District.

Earl C. Elliott
Served as president of California Water Service Company from 1929 to 1939. He was chairman of the board from 1939 to April 1941 and continued as a director until his retirement in 1948.

Elliott was well-qualified for his new position, bringing to the table a wealth of managerial and water works experience. A 1900 engineering graduate of DePauw University, he had been a vice president of the Wichita (Kansas) Water Company and later, city manager of Wichita. A native of Kokomo, Indiana, Elliott's earlier background in water utility management had been well-grounded. He was vice president and manager of the Kokomo Water Works Company, president of the Mt. Vernon (Indiana) Electric Light and Power Co. and assistant secretary of the Muncie Water Works Company.

Several years into his tenure as president of Cal Water, Elliott assumed a dual role as head of Federal's Oregon-Washington subsidiary. He served as Cal Water president for more than a decade until Federal Water sold its California subsidiary to General Water, Gas and Electric Co. in 1939. Under the new ownership, Elliott would serve as chairman of the board until April of 1941.

Chapter 7

What a hectic place to work...

The country's tumultuous growth in the 1920s came to an abrupt end on *Black Thursday*, Oct. 24, 1929, the day the New York Stock Exchange crashed and prices tumbled. More than $4 billion in stock value was lost in a single day as panic raged on the floor of the Exchange. A visitor from California remembered the day well.

Twenty-nine-year-old Fred Dodge, manager of Cal Water's East Los Angeles District, had been summoned back to New York to attend training sessions at the New York headquarters of Federal Water Service Company. Dodge, a native of the Los Angeles area, was the only one among the Federal people who had knowledge about activities in southern California.

On the day he toured the New York Stock Exchange, Dodge did not realize that the market was in the midst of its history-making downward spiral that would mark the beginning of The Great Depression. As he watched pandemonium raging on the exchange floor below, with people hysterically yelling and scurrying about, Dodge thought to himself, *"How lucky I am not to work every day in such a hectic place."*

He later explained how he finally understood the anguish of that day in 1929 when he actually witnessed the suicide of a distraught investor leaping from a New York highrise. Ironically, the main purpose of the training sessions was to instruct Dodge and the other utility managers on selling and promoting stock in a new holding company being organized by Federal Water's George Ohrstrom. The new venture, Utility Operators Company, would become the parent company of Federal Water Service, whose own stock was being used as collateral for the new holding company. However, with the stock market crashing, there was no public market for the new company and consequently, Dodge and the other Federal managers were urged to go back home and gain cooperation of their employees to sell stock in the Utility Operators Company. The employees themselves would be asked to buy shares on the payroll deduction plan. Years later when the Utility Operators Co. had been liquidated, shares of its subsidiary companies were distributed to the employees who had bought stock, even though the shares essentially had no market value at the time. Because of the ill will that these stock transactions had created among the early workers, it would be almost 50 years before California Water Service would consider offering Company stock for sale to its employees.

Unfortunately, for many of the shareholders of holding companies with electric, gas and water utilities as subsidiaries, the stock market crash resulted in the loss of billions of dollars. Many of the operating utilities had been purchased at inflated prices by their holding companies and were operating at a loss as profits were funneled back to the parent company.

Fortunately, California Water Service Company was one of the more profitable operations in Federal's conglomerate of utility companies, and despite the precarious economic conditions of the Depression, the Company would continue to grow and prosper.

Chapter 8

"So, if someone comes along...
Call the police!"

Municipal ownership attempts on Federal's West Coast properties plagued the Company from its very beginning. In the Oregon-Washington Water subsidiary, the City of Hoquiam in Washington State won a judgment of condemnation in September of 1929, allowing the City to take control of the water system. The decree was set aside while the Company continued its battle through the courts to derail the City takeover. But the Company's most significant municipal threat would occur in the California Fresno District.

City efforts to acquire the Company's Fresno water operations had begun almost immediately after Federal had purchased the system in 1926. During the next four years, city officials conducted an aggressive campaign to win control of the local water properties. As previously noted, the Fresno City Water Company was serving as Cal Water's first statewide General Office and was the source of its top executive talent.

As soon as word circulated that New York interests had bought the water operations in Fresno, the community became enraged. Rumors spread throughout the City that the new owners were planning to install water meters throughout the residential community. There had been a long tradition in Fresno supporting a policy that provided homeowners flat-rate service.* The Company vehemently

---

A tradition that survived a ballot measure in 2000 that residents rejected calling for voluntary reading of residential meters.

denied that residential metering was being considered. Thus, even before the Federal people had time to take off their coats to begin work, a four-year battle with the city ensued for control of the water company.

In a January 8, 1930 editorial, the *Fresno Republican* commented...

> *"The citizens of Fresno should never let any one persuade them that water ownership is a matter of mere business shrewdness. Fresno should and must own its own water supply because of the need of permanent control and of permanent enterprise. Water ownership is vital to life in California. In so far as the State of California and Federal laws of the United States permit, the City of Fresno should gain control of the resources and the mechanism of water supply.*
>
> *"So, if someone comes along and offers us some smart bargain by which we are to be diverted from a public water control policy, call the police. There is something wrong with any proposal to get us, for some few cents' advantage, to turn our hand from our own water salvation."*

On Jan. 14, 1930, the California Supreme Court denied Cal Water's petition to review the decision of the California Railroad Commission, which had set $2,327,000 as a fair price to be paid by Fresno for the Company's city water system. The Company maintained that the Commission had exceeded its jurisdiction in fixing the valuation and that the constitutional rights of the Company were injured. The Company had set a price of $3,027,000. Since the community and city officials had been concerned about the possibility of water meters being placed on residential services, Cal Water's president, Earl Elliott, made a last-minute offer. He told the City that the

Company would not install meters or increase rates in the near future if the City agreed to drop all proceedings to acquire the water works. Further, Elliott promised that if the condemnation matter was dropped, he would spend the money that had been set aside for court costs for "improvements in the physical properties of the Company in Fresno."

The City stood fast in its demands, refusing both to accept Elliott's offer and to drop its condemnation efforts to acquire the local water system. With no other options available, the Company was forced to negotiate and complete the sale of the Fresno system, effective Feb. 1, 1931. Fresno would be the only California system that Federal was forced to relinquish during its 13-year period of ownership of California Water Service Company.

Despite Elliott's aggressive attempts to retain Fresno, he soon learned that the New York holding company's interests were not at all displeased with the outcome. The Fresno sale was a bonanza in their eyes, reaping nearly $2 million in cash to reinvest. The sum was a substantial amount in those days as the economic woes of the Depression continued both for the nation and for the utility holding companies. However, the benefit of this new-found wealth for the Federal holding company was short-lived. Much to the dismay of the eastern stockholders, the California Railroad Commission quickly stepped into the picture, ordering that the proceeds from the Fresno sale be reinvested in California. The Fresno funds were not about to leave the California economy.

Faced with this prospect, Chenery and Elliott agreed that a substantial part of the proceeds should be used to establish the Company in one of northern California's primary growth areas. On July 17, 1931, the Company acquired the service districts of the Pacific Water Company, which were located immediately south of the City of

San Francisco in an area known as the San Francisco Peninsula. These properties included the water systems serving South San Francisco, San Mateo, Lomita Park (adjacent to the town of Millbrae), and portions of Hillsborough. Acquired on that same date were two additional Peninsula water systems — the San Carlos Water Company and the Los Altos Water Company.

Joe Viguier, a utility worker for the Pacific Company, joined Cal Water and began a distinguished 44-year career with the Company, serving as purchasing agent, general manager and, finally, vice president of operations and construction before his retirement in 1975.

By the end of 1931, the Company would lay claim to being the largest privately owned water utility on the Pacific Coast with service to 73,000 customers in California, from Redding in the north to Los Angeles in the south. It served the communities of:

Redondo Beach	Port Costa
Hermosa Beach	Concord
East Los Angeles	Crockett
Bakersfield	Danville
Visalia	Martinez (wholesale)
Hanford	Valona (near Crockett)
Stockton	Walnut Creek (wholesale)
Livermore	Petaluma
So. San Francisco	Marysville
Lomita Park	Chico
Hillsborough (portion)	Oroville
San Carlos	Dixon
Los Altos	Redding
Willows	Port Chicago
San Mateo	

The Company also directed a major part of the Fresno proceeds that year toward improvements in its Contra Costa County District. Lacking a sufficient long-range water supply for the area, Cal Water undertook construction of the Chenery Project, the largest water project in Company history until recent times. The project would fall under the direction of Trojan Engineers, a San Francisco-based subsidiary organization established by Chenery in 1929. The firm had been staffed by newly hired engineers to serve the needs of California Water Service Company and other clients. Kirby Barnum, Cal Water's chief engineer, would also serve as president and chief engineer of the Trojan Company.

Centerpiece of the Chenery Project was a one-billion-gallon reservoir built near the Naval Weapons Station and the City of Concord on a Company-owned site known as the Government Ranch off Highway 4.

During the winter and spring, a water supply was pumped into the reservoir from the Mallard Slough near Antioch when rain and Sierra runoff created fresh water flood flows into Suisun Bay. Approximately 22 million gallons of water were pumped daily from the Bay through the Company's Mallard Pumping Station. A 42-inch steel and concrete pipeline transported the water 5 1/2 miles to the reservoir, thus storing the district's supply for the summer months.

In geographic terms, the Contra Costa District was the Company's largest, serving communities within an area covering approximately 200 square miles. To the north, customers were located in Crockett, Martinez and Port Chicago along the San Francisco Estuary and Suisun Bay. The Company service area extended south to the communities of Concord and Walnut Creek and down through the San Ramon Valley. The Town of Danville became the Company's southern boundary in Contra Costa County following purchase of that community's water company on Aug. 31, 1931.

Recognizing the potential for customer growth in Contra Costa, the Company also made significant improvements along the San Ramon Valley corridor.

In April of 1931, a major transmission line was completed, connecting the Company's filter plant at the Chenery Reservoir to the south county service areas. The 10-mile transmission line brought surface water supply to Concord retail customers and wholesale supply to Walnut Creek. It provided surface water supply to Danville and to the extensive development that was taking place in the nearby Mt. Diablo Country Club area. Ranchers and homeowners along the pipeline were also taking service. The Company officials would note that:

"The new transmission facilities allowed for an adequate supply of excellent water to serve all valley customers" and that *"the Company's entry into the San Ramon Valley was enthusiastically received by the residents."* The Company predicted at the time that the new source of water would bring rapid and substantial development to the area.

With completion of the Chenery Project in 1932, the Trojan Engineers subsidiary would disband as a result of economic conditions created by the Depression. When Cal Water came under new ownership in 1939, the Chenery Project, including the reservoir and treatment plant, would be renamed for the area's nearby Mallard Slough. The Mallard Project would augment the Company's water supply needs in the Contra Costa District for the next 20 years.

This 1929 photograph of Cal Water's District staff in Stockton was taken in front of the original commercial office on Sutter Street. As the senior member of a father-son team, Epitasio Castanon, third from left in front row, would retire from Cal Water after serving 31 years. His Company service was later followed by that of his son, Rito, who would serve the Company as a field worker for 39 years. Most of the employees shown were with PG&E's water operations in Stockton when it was purchased by Cal Water in 1927.

Hard hats were not in style during this 1929 pipe-laying project in the Contra Costa District.

In this circa 1930 photograph, California Water Service Company representatives tour the construction site of the Chenery Reservoir, a Company supply source for the Contra Costa District. Included in the group is Thomas H. Wiggin, right, a founding partner of California Water Service and prominent utility engineer. Others shown are, from left, Oswald Spier, Cal Water engineer; E. K. Barnum, vice president and chief engineer; H.K. Griffin, northern division manager; Earl C. Elliott, president, and Bucky Harris (behind Wiggin), future chief engineer for the Company.

In this May 1930 photograph, East Los Angeles District employees, proudly exhibit their sign-up sheets listing newly subscribed shareholders in Federal Water's new holding company, the Utility Operators Company. The employees were winners in a contest to sell the most shares of stock. Standing by at right, is Fred Dodge, manager of the East Los Angeles District and future Cal Water president and Board member.

Jeptha A. Wade, Sr.
Chief engineer for California Water Service Company from 1933 to 1944. A native of Michigan, he had joined the parent company, Federal Water Service, in 1928, serving on Federal's executive engineering staff in the East under Thomas Wiggin. His son, Jeptha A. Wade, Jr., became chief engineer in 1966.

Chapter 9

The General Office finds new
and stately quarters...

Prior to the Fresno sale, President Elliott had recognized the need to consolidate General Office operations in San Francisco, which would require moving from the Hunter-Dulin Building to larger quarters. Offices on the fifth floor of the stately San Francisco Federal Reserve Bank Building, 400 Sansome Street at Sacramento Street, were selected for the Company's new headquarters. The bank building would serve as the Cal Water General Office for more than a decade until its move to San Jose in 1940.

As the Company entered the Depression Decade, it reported that 1931 had been a good year financially, despite the adverse economic conditions prevailing throughout the nation. Adding to the difficulties of the period was a severe, seven-year drought, one of the longest known in California history. However, Company officials noted that with customer cooperation in saving water, it had not been necessary to place restrictions upon use, thus *"enabling the Company to meet its service obligations promptly and adequately."*

At year's end, it was announced that the parent company, Federal Water Service Company, was in control of the largest group of privately owned water systems in the United States after only six years in operation. In addition to California Water Service Company and the Oregon-Washington Water Service Company, its subsidiaries included the Scranton (Pennsylvania) Water Works, the Long Island Water Company, the Birmingham Gas Company and the Scranton (Ohio)

Water Company. Federal was listed as a unit of the Tri-Utilities System of public utility properties valued at more than $320 million.

Except for the Company's effort to revisit the possible purchase of the San Jose Water Works later in the year, Elliott had decided to curtail any acquisition efforts in 1932. Such was the decision despite numerous opportunities being offered. Because of the current economic conditions, Elliott felt he could not justify the assumption of any new obligations, preferring rather to conserve the Company's credit rating for other purposes.

During the year, Dean Witter, founder of Dean Witter & Co. in San Francisco, was elected to the Cal Water Board. This brought the number of directors to seven including:

Christopher T. Chenery, chairman of the Board and
    president of Federal Water Service Co.

Earl C. Elliott, president of California Water Service Company

A. Crawford Green, Sr. and

Warren Olney, Jr., attorneys for McCutchen, Olney,
    Mannon and Greene

 Russell Lowry, vice president of the American Trust
    Company, San Francisco

E. B. Walthall, vice president, California Water Service Company

Dean Witter, founder, Dean Witter & Co.

Except for Chenery and Elliott, who were the Federal Water Service Company representatives on the Board, all other members were "local" directors from San Francisco.

Chapter 10

"I don't know how hot this thing is..."

By the fall of 1932, it appeared that Chenery had once again placed the San Jose Water deal back on the table. On Oct. 10, 1932, Chenery wrote Elliott:

"My Dear Earl:

...I do not know whether anything is going to develop out of San Jose (Water Works) or not. I should be glad to have it for $4,600,000 but am not inclined to go higher than that for it. Of course, we would have, in addition to that, the discount on the bonds which might run it up to $4,900,000."

By this time, Chenery was dealing with his old adversary in the holding company business, P. M. Chandler, president of General Water, Gas and Electric. Both had vied to gain control of San Jose Water Works in 1929. At that time, Chandler was the winner in acquiring the San Jose water company. By July of 1933 it appeared that an agreement could be reached between Federal's Chenery and General's Chandler for a Cal Water purchase of San Jose Water. Chenery sent a telegram on July 6 to Earl Elliott in San Francisco stating that he was meeting with Chandler in New York and felt that the sale would go through if Cal Water's directors approved the purchase agreement. Chenery asked Elliott to provide him with his views on the proposed acquisition.

Even though Cal Water was a Federal subsidiary, Elliott's response to Chenery on the proposed purchase indicated that the California management was no rubber stamp, not hesitant to express its concerns regarding the proposed deal to buy San Jose Water Works. On July 6, 1933, Elliott wrote Chenery:

"Dear Mr. Chenery:

I have your wire of today giving a brief outline of the program you think you might be able to work out with Mr. Chandler for the acquisition of San Jose (Water Works). We have spent the afternoon analyzing the suggestion and the following just about represents the viewpoint of those of us who are in this office. Dean Witter, Judge Olney and Crawford Greene (Cal Water Board members) are out of town so we have been unable to discuss the suggestion with any members of the California Board. I hope to get in touch with Dean Witter, Judge (Warren) Olney and (Russell) Lowry on Monday when we have a meeting of the California Board...

"We are not clear on the price that is being discussed. There are a number of features in Mr. Chandler's suggestion which strike us as objectionable. One or two of them would appear to be a bar to the consummation of a deal."

Elliott explained that the Cal Water management was not confident in just assuming that the Railroad Commission would approve a sale at $5,000,000. He explained to Chenery that it was their feeling that the Commission would fix a net price at a figure approximating a condemnation price somewhere between $4,000,000 and $4,250,000. Elliott also expressed concern that the Chandler proposal would turn over to General Water 10,000 shares of Cal Water's preferred stock and 10,000 shares of the common stock that Federal Water presently controlled. This would result in Chandler holding 20,000 voting shares against 14,142 voting shares in the hands of Federal.

Cal Water management, Elliott explained, expressed concern that

Chenery and Federal would automatically lose control of the California property. Elliott wrote to his superior that this *"was an insurmountable objection."* Finally, Elliott and his Cal Water management were reluctant to see an additional series of California bonds issued with a higher rate than those that were presently outstanding in the hands of the public. The California team felt that an additional series of bonds under such conditions would have a detrimental effect on the price of the outstanding bonds and probably would also have an adverse effect on the Company's credit.

It was Elliott's feeling that a very vigorous protest would be made against such an issue by the Company's present fiscal agent. In concluding his remarks to Chenery, Elliott wrote:

"We, of course, would like to see San Jose (Water Works) come into the California picture. But, like you, we want to see it come in only in such a way that you and we will have the maximum protection and reap the maximum benefit. Under the suggestion that has been made to you we think that is impossible. I do not know how hot this thing is, but I wish that it could be held off until you get out here so that you can discuss this matter frankly and freely with the California Board. It is of such importance that it is going to be extremely difficult to keep the California Board informed and to give them an opportunity to develop their views otherwise. You know the new Securities Act puts a good deal of responsibility on individual members of boards of directors and these folks out here are going to feel some natural reluctance to approving a transaction with which they are not thoroughly familiar. It is imperative that some action be taken in this matter before you get to California and have an opportunity to discuss the situation out here. I believe it is of sufficient importance to

justify my bringing one member of the California Board East.

Yours Truly,

Earl C. Elliott"

Elliott followed with a letter to Cal Water Board member Crawford Greene, who was on vacation at the time, explaining his communications on the San Jose Water acquisition matter with Chenery in New York:

July 11, 1933

"Dear Crawford:

On Saturday night Mr. Chenery called me from Winsted at my home and said the matter was awfully hot. I concluded from his conversation that the boys (Chenery's backers) in New York were giving him the rush act. He may be giving it to himself, or at least making himself peculiarly susceptible to pressure. I asked him to wait until he could have some con-versation out here on the subject and he didn't seem to be very anxious to do that. I told him we had objections and I knew that the Board would want to discuss the matter.

"As I think you know, Mr. Chenery expects to be here on Saturday, the 22nd. He expects to spend Saturday, Sunday and Monday here (in San Francisco) and then go south to Visalia to climb Mt. Whitney. I want to have him have a conference with the California Board on Monday, July 24th. I don't know what your plans are, but Mr. Chenery suggested in one of his letters that you might go up on Mt. Whitney with him. If that is true, I hope you can be present at the conference on Monday.

"Don't let all this junk get on your mind or give you a lot of worry. The situation is such now that I am very sure Mr. Chenery would not think of committing on the matter until after he had

a personal conversation with the California Board.

Sincerely,

Earl C. Elliott"

It is not known to what extent the opposition of the California Board and management may have influenced the final outcome, but the acquisition by Cal Water was never consummated and General Water would continue its ownership of San Jose Water Works as a subsidiary until 1945.

The Federal Reserve Bank Building (The Old Fed) at 400 Sansome Street, San Francisco, served as the Company's General Office for more than a decade before the move in 1940 to San Jose. The Company's offices were on the fifth floor, directly above the portico columns. The building was constructed in 1924 and is now included in the National Register of Historical Places.

Chapter 11

"We left town, our tail between our legs..."

A year following the forced sale of its Fresno District in 1931, Cal Water faced the first of five more municipal takeover attempts during the decade. One action would eventually result in the loss of another Cal Water system.

In May of 1932, the City of Visalia had sought approval by its citizens for a $250,000 bond issue to purchase Cal Water's system with valuation set by the California Railroad Commission in a city condemnation action. The community's vote to reject the City's purchase attempt by a 3 to 1 margin would portend a pattern of strong customer support for Cal Water in combating future statewide municipal assaults. Within two years of the Visalia vote, the City of Redding sought community approval for bonds to finance purchase of the Company's local water system. Once again, voters resoundingly defeated the measure by a 10 to 1 margin. An effort by the City of Redondo Beach to win approval for bonds to purchase the water system also was rejected by the community in October of 1936. The City was to receive a grant from the Federal Public Works Administration to help cover the cost.

The following year Cal Water was again confronted with a public ownership threat, this time in the community of Menlo Park on the San Francisco Peninsula. The ballot measure, seeking to form a public water district in the area, was overwhelmingly defeated on Aug. 17, 1937.

Officials in the City of Redding, however, finally prevailed in their efforts to win voter support for condemnation bonds in early 1937. Once again, supplemental funding totaling $162,000 was offered by the federal government to augment the $200,000 bond issue that was approved by voters. Redding's venture into the retail water business would precipitate one of the most bizarre episodes in Cal Water history. With the bond proceeds and federal grant funds in City hands by October of 1937, the Company made attempts to negotiate a sale of its water system. But local officials rejected the idea and proceeded with plans to build their own water plant throughout the City.

The Company took immediate legal action to prevent the duplication effort and a temporary Federal Court restraining order was granted. However, in February of 1938, the U.S District Court dismissed the Company's case, lifting the restraining order. In the meantime, the City continued to rebuke all Company efforts to negotiate a sale and it now appeared that the City of Redding would have two water works systems operating in competition. Cal Water's total annual income from the Redding District at the time was approximately $52,000. The Cal Water Board instructed Company President Earl Elliott to travel to Washington, D. C. in an attempt to persuade the Public Works Administration to reconsider their grant to the City, but unfortunately, his effort was to no avail.

The federal government at the time was constructing Shasta Dam some 15 miles north of the City where many of the project's workers were living. Officials in the U.S. Interior Department had given their blessings to the federal grant *"to provide a newer and upgraded water system to the City for the benefit of the workers."* By May of 1939, Redding was in full operation with a city-owned water system in competition with Cal Water. The City had completely duplicated the Company's distribution system within the community!

Cal Water initially lost half of its customer base, or 908 consumers, who had signed up to receive water from the City. By the end of the year, the Company had 900 active Redding services generating $32,771 in annual gross income, compared to 1,013 customers who had signed up for service from the City's competing water works. Cal Water's Joe Viguier was ordered to Redding with a Company sales team from San Mateo with a plan to go door to door, soliciting residents to re-sign as Cal Water customers. After competing with the City's water system for 27 months, the Company was finally forced to call it quits. As one observer would recall, "We left town with our tail between our legs."

As required, the Company made an application to the California Railroad Commission to suspend service to the community. Both the City and Cal Water had been operating at a loss with each serving approximately 50% of the total water customers in the City. Cal Water was forced to sell its property to the City at "junk" value in the amount of $27,500 with the sale taking place in August of 1941, resulting in a loss to the Company of $204,240. The Redding episode had been particularly disturbing for the Company because of the participation by the federal government in providing the City with substantial grant funding to help build the competing system.

A quarter of a century later, the saga of the Company's Redding fiasco would resurface. The episode was referenced in 1964 as part of the successful effort by the private water industry in California to win state approval of the so-called Service Duplication Law. Senate Bill 687, which passed into law in 1965, allowed for just compensation to a private utility if a governmental agency chose to duplicate any portion of the utility's operating plant. Compensation would provide not only for the value of the facilities lost, but also for the revenue potential of the vacated facilities.

Employees of the Bakersfield District gather for this equipment training session conducted by The Mueller Company representative standing third from right. Among those Cal Water employees identified in this circa 1931 photograph are, back row, left to right, Si Dillon, district manager; Howard Finch, chief clerk, John Dillon, counter clerk; and second from right, Ed Baldwin, district bookkeeper. Front row kneeling, second from left, Roy Payne, service installer; fourth from left, Doc Roberts, service installer; Edwin Andersen, student summer relief clerk and future Stockton district manager; Willie Guy Foster, pump operator; Hemp Peavy, pump operator.

The Company's 25,000-gallon tank provided water storage for the Crockett service area in the early days of the Contra Costa District. Shown in the background is the ongoing construction of the Carquinez Bridge.

Chapter 12

Reining in the holding companies...

B y 1935, with Cal Water's statewide customer totals reaching 68,473, personnel changes were taking place that would have significant impact on the future management of the Company. Fred Dodge, East Los Angeles district manager since 1927, was brought into the General Office in San Francisco with Laurence Camy, one of the original Fresno Water alumni, replacing him in East Los Angeles.

Earlier, Chenery had sent out from New York one of his top engineers, Jeptha A. Wade, Sr., to become chief engineer for the California company. Wade, who would serve 11 years as chief engineer for Cal Water until his death in 1944, had been employed by Federal Water Service Company since 1926, serving as assistant chief engineer of Federal's eastern properties under Thomas Wiggin.

His son, Jeptha A. Wade, Jr., whose own Cal Water career would span more than 40 years, served the Company as vice president for 25 years and, like his father, as chief engineer, a position he held from 1966 to 1987. The senior Wade was a grandnephew of Jeptha H. Wade, the founder and first president of the Pacific Telegraph Company, which eventually became Pacific Bell, now a subsidiary of SBC Corp.

During 1935, the American States Public Service Company was going through bankruptcy proceedings and Chenery had sought to acquire one of its properties, the Southern California Water Company, through an offer to the Reorganization Committee. General Water, Gas and Electric eventually won out over Chenery in the acquisition effort, and took possession of the southern California company. But Chenery would pursue the purchase of Southern California Water Company again in 1937, this time dealing with its new owner, P.M. Chandler, president of General Water, his old adversary. The offer was presented at a luncheon meeting in New York in September with Cal Water's eastern securities expert George Ohrstrom in attendance, but once again Chenery's acquisition attempt would be thwarted.

That same year, General Water would entice out of retirement a nationally known utility executive, Ralph Elsman, to head up its national operations. He assumed leadership of the 38 water utilities throughout the country controlled by General Water, while becoming president of both Southern California Water Company and San Jose Water Works. Ironically, it would be Ralph Elsman who would become president of California Water Service Company in 1939 upon its own acquisition by Chandler and the General Water, Gas and Electric Company.

Meanwhile, by the mid-1930s, Federal's subsidiary serving the northwest had changed its name to the Peoples Water and Gas Company (formerly Oregon-Washington Water Service Company). Previously, the Oregon-Washington Water Service Company had been managed by Cal Water personnel. Except for contract services provided by Cal Water's chief engineer and its water quality department, the two subsidiaries would operate under separate management from this point forward.

By 1935, the federal government had taken steps to deal with the stock market abuses in the utility industry with Congress adopting the Public Utility Holding Company Act (PUHCA, pronounced "Puh Ca"). The new law was directed chiefly toward gas and electric holding companies.

A primary concern had centered around questionable marketing activities of certain gas and electric utility holding companies in the sale of stock to the general public. Federal Water Service Company, Cal Water's parent company, itself was a subsidiary of the Utility Operators Company, whose acquisition and marketing practices had raised the ire of federal agencies. With passage of the new law, Cal Water President Earl Elliott sought to determine how his Company would be affected, being a subsidiary of Federal Water. He learned from his legal advisors that Cal Water, as a utility company engaged solely in the water business, was not considered to be a public utility company within the meaning of PUHCA. Likewise, Federal Water would not be considered a holding company under the Act because of its water utility holdings. However, since Federal Water was also the parent of gas and electric subsidiaries, it would be required to register as a holding company under terms of the new legislation. Consequently, Cal Water, as a Federal subsidiary, would be subject to certain conditions imposed by PUHCA. To be in compliance, Company attorneys recommended to Cal Water: *"Eliminate certain practices by which the services of your chief engineer and the facilities of your laboratory were made available to the Peoples Water and Gas Company"* (formerly the Oregon-Washington Water Service Company and also a subsidiary of Federal Water).

By December 1937, attorneys advised Elliott that Cal Water, as a Federal Water subsidiary, was exempt from all provisions of PUHCA, including the latest amendments. Cal Water, however, was required to comply with all federal Securities and Exchange Commission rules involving acquisitions and company reorganization.

The Company's service area on the San Francisco Peninsula was expanded on June 15, 1936, with the purchase of Bear Gulch Water Company from the University of California, the first major acquisition by Cal Water since 1931. The Bear Gulch system, located on the southern edge of San Mateo County, served 2,000 consumers in the communities of Menlo Park, Atherton, Woodside and nearby unincorporated areas. A portion of the proceeds from a $10,000,000 bond sale that year were used to purchase the Bear Gulch property, which was valued at $1 million.

During that same year, Cal Water agreed to accommodate the Peninsula town of Hillsborough by selling to the town a portion of the Company's water system serving 200 customers, approximately one-third of the community. Citizens of the community had voted to approve the sale of bonds to purchase the seven different existing utility systems that were serving the town, thus creating a unified operation.

In the nearby Peninsula community of San Mateo, Cal Water would construct a $50,000 lime and soda ash softening plant that year to treat well water in the community. It was believed that the new installation was the first lime and soda plant on the Pacific Coast to be built exclusively for the softening of a public water supply, marking the beginning of a long line of water quality innovations pioneered by Cal Water.

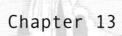

Chapter 13

The changing of the guard...

With the passage of PUHCA, Chenery had determined it would be necessary to reorganize his holding company by selling his West Coast water utilities to be in compliance with the new law.

In 1939, he once again met at the negotiating table with P.M. Chandler of General Water, and by August it was announced that Federal Water Service Company, which owned all the common stock of California Water Service Company, had sold its entire holdings to General Water, Gas and Electric Company of New York.

Chenery would continue to operate Federal Water Service Company for a time, but his activities would eventually focus on his gas company holdings. He had been chairman of the board of Southern Natural Gas Company and the Off Shore Company with valuable holdings below the surface in the sea belt off the Gulf of Mexico. Today, Southern Natural Gas Company is based in Birmingham, Alabama, and is a subsidiary of the El Paso Corporation, the largest natural gas company in the world.

The change in ownership of Cal Water would also herald the arrival of 54-year-old Ralph Elsman, utility executive extraordinaire, whose tenure as chief executive would shape the destiny of the Company during the next two decades. In 1936, Elsman had surfaced from a self-imposed, 10-year retirement to become executive vice president of General Water, Gas and Electric, serving directly under P.M. Chandler. Elsman had been given the responsibility at General Water to reorganize that Company's management, sell off many of its underlying properties and, in general, ensure the Company was conforming to the newly created Public Utility Holding Company Act.

His responsibilities on behalf of General Water were so broad in scope as to indicate Chandler's total confidence and respect in his new executive. Elsman traveled frequently between his West Coast base in San Jose and New York, overseeing General Water's numerous utility holdings throughout the country while continuing to serve as president of General's two major California operating companies, San Jose Water Works and Southern California Water Company. Further, Chandler demonstrated such trust in Elsman's abilities and reputation, he appointed him to serve as a director or officer in many of General's national holdings and affiliations.*

By 1939, the financial interests controlling General Water had split the Company into two entities, with Elsman remaining with the Chandler faction out of Brooklyn, New York and continuing on as president of San Jose Water Works. Elsman's executive plate, however, was heaped full again that August when he was called upon by Chandler to head the operations of his latest acquisition, California Water Service Company.

*Elsman's affiliations on behalf of General Water included Dominion Gas & Electric Co., Wilmington, DE.; General Water, Gas and Electric Co., NY, NY; Boise Water Corp., Boise, ID; Capital City Water Co., Jefferson City, MO; Consolidated Company of Utica, Utica, NY; Freeport Water Co., Freeport, PA; Indiana Water Works Co., Greensburg, IN; Jersey Shore Water Company, Jersey Shore, PA; Lloydell Water Co., Johnstown, PA; Natatorium Company, Boise, ID; Nippenose Water Co., Lycoming Co., PA; Portage Water Co., Portage, PA; Porter Water Co., Porter, PA; Pinellas Water Co., St. Petersburg, FL; Rockland Gas Co., Inc., Suffern, NY; Selladasburg Water Co., Salladasburg, PA; San Jose Water Works, San Jose, CA; Sedalia Water Company, Sedalia, MO; Southern Water Company, St. Petersburg, FL; Tiadaghton Water Co., Pine Creek Township, PA; Utica City Ice Co., Utica, NY; Winchester Water Works Co., Wilmington, DE; American States Utilities, Wilmington, DE; Southern California Water Co., Los Angeles, CA; Grimes Pass Power Co., Grimes Pass, ID; Hermiston Light and Power Co., Hermiston, OR; Kellogg Water Co., Kellogg, ID; Rathdrum Power Co., ID; International Utilities Corp., NY, NY.

Ralph Elsman...Utility Executive Extraordinaire
*Left photo: Shown here during his seventies, Elsman's dynamic
utility career would span a period of 68 years! His 21 years at the
helm of California Water Service enabled the Company to achieve
prominence as one of the nation's premier water utilities.
Right photo: Retiring for the first time in 1925, a multi-millionaire
at age 40, Elsman had already won high recognition and respect
throughout the utility industry before joining Cal Water in 1939.*

Chapter 14

He knew his calling...

Cal Water once again fell under the influence of eastern interests. But the selection of Ralph Elsman as president could not have brought the Company a more experienced, eminent and respected utility executive. His 21-year reign as Cal Water's chief executive would have significant and long-lasting impact, although during his distinguished career with the Company, he would encounter numerous challenges and adversities, including personal tragedies that would strike him and his family.

He was born in New Haven, Connecticut, on July 22, 1885. His father had died before his birth and his mother had given him up for adoption to her parents, who bestowed upon him their family name, Elsman. He spent his early childhood in Mt. Vernon, New York, living with his maternal grandparents and attending local schools, where his prowess in baseball as a star on the Mt. Vernon High School team had attracted the attention of the community and, more importantly, of officials at the Westchester Lighting Company. He was hired by the company when he was only 15 years old and still in high school. He loved the sport of baseball and reportedly had been offered the opportunity to play professionally in the Texas League, but according to his daughter, Nancy Elsman Pierce, it seemed her father knew his calling was the public utility business.

While still in high school, he had left his grandparents' home to make his own way by working part-time for the lighting company, first doing janitorial work and later, shoveling coal in the company's electric generating plant in Brooklyn. Upon graduation from high school at age 17, he became a cadet engineer for the Westchester Company, which was recognized at that time as a pioneer in the distribution of electrical power in suburban areas of New York. During the next several years, he would advance from office boy to the company's superintendent of plants in Westchester County at the age of 21. It was during this period that he had his memorable meeting with John D. Rockefeller, Sr., back in 1905.

In 1907, he was offered a job in Alaska to construct an electric light plant in the community of Whitehorse in the Yukon Territory. After he had arrived in San Francisco en route to Alaska, he would learn that the project had been abandoned. With no funds and alone in San Francisco, he was able to secure employment with Pacific Gas & Electric Company, which was being formed at the time and acquiring properties throughout northern and central California. He was placed in charge of PG&E's construction crews in Marysville, Colusa, Chico, Napa, Petaluma and Santa Rosa. Later he directed construction of the company's underground system of power lines in downtown San Jose. Prophetically, he would return to these environs a quarter of a century later as president and chief executive of San Jose Water Works and California Water Service Company.

During his employment with PG&E, Elsman demonstrated his inventive talents by creating a device known as the *Elsman Three-Phase 11,000-volt Combination Air Switch and Fuse*. It was a multi-word designation for an important invention of the time. The device would reduce to one-third the cost of an antiquated switch that had been manufactured by General Electric. It would also reduce costs and increase efficiency in the use of electrical power for irrigation in the San Joaquin Valley and Contra Costa County. His compensation for the patent was just one dollar!

In 1915, Elsman made the decision to leave PG&E and California and return to New York. There he was named general manager of the Kings County Lighting Company, which served an area of two-million residents in Brooklyn and Queens County. He was elected president in 1918, and it was during his tenure with the Kings County company that Elsman became nationally known for appearing on the cover of *Forbes* magazine in 1920 at the ripe old age of 35.

When Elsman took command of the Kings County Lighting Company, the utility was faced with several million dollars in back taxes. Although the company was the third largest gas and electric company in New York State, the burden of delinquent taxes coupled with political difficulties had placed the firm on the verge of collapse. Throughout this period of trauma, Elsman would encourage his employees never to forget the importance of maintaining customer service. He passed on to them the paramount rule of the public utility business he had learned early in his career... *"that dependable service to the consumer always came first."*

The company's financial straits made it impossible for Elsman to receive meaningful cash compensation as president, and he agreed to be paid partially in company bonds. After a time, his holdings became substantial, and he would add to his position by investing in more company bonds, which at that time were selling for about 10 cents on the dollar.

Using his own financial reputation to hold off foreclosures by creditors, Elsman proceeded to acquire controlling interest in the troubled company by borrowing $150,000 from New York financier Charles Dickey, a man he had never met. In order to secure the six-month loan, Elsman put the company's assets up as collateral and offered Dickey a bonus of 2,500 shares in the Kings County Lighting

Company. As was his life-long practice, Elsman repaid the loan promptly...within 30 days.

Meanwhile, other uses for gas were being invented, including its need for cooking purposes. Soon, the value of the company and its holdings began to skyrocket, and Elsman was sitting atop a gold mine. His steadfast efforts to preserve his credit standing as well as his reputation throughout the banking and utility communities would prove to be a monumental asset for California Water Service Company in later years.

In 1925, Elsman sold his interest in the Kings County Lighting Company and retired a multi-millionaire at age 40, moving to Nevada where he purchased a 7,000-acre ranch in Washoe County above Carson City. He built and maintained a second home on Kennedy Road in Los Gatos, California.

Elsman continued in retirement for more than a decade before he was offered the executive position with General Water, Gas and Electric in 1936. In a 1999 interview, Nancy Elsman Pierce, his daughter, provided a personal insight into the character and personality of her father:

"My dad had a wonderful reputation...He really didn't care whether he was well-liked or not, as long as his family and his good friends loved him. But as far as business went, being a well-liked, enjoyable boss, he was not. My dad was more interested in being respected. He had a wonderful rapport with all the bankers he ever dealt with in San Francisco. When he first came out to California, he met Will Crocker of Crocker Bank and they became good friends, and he could borrow millions of dollars from Will Crocker with just a handshake. And my dad always paid it off. He was a very independent person, very motivated, iron-willed. He would tell us that he always knew he was going to make a success of himself. He would instill in us

thoughts of confidence and determination all the time. He would say, 'Don't let any habit get the best of you....always be in control.'"

When Christopher Chenery and Federal Water Service Company relinquished ownership in August of 1939, Elsman basically retained the existing Cal Water Board of Directors. Earl Elliott, who had served as Chenery's president for the past ten years, was elevated to chairman of the Board. P.M. Chandler, president of General Water, and Elsman, both of whom represented the interests of the holding company, became directors. The remaining Board members, all local Bay Area residents, included A. Crawford Greene, Sr. of McCutchen; Russell Lowry of the American Trust Co., Oakland; Dean Witter of the Dean Witter Co., San Francisco; and E.B. Walthall, vice president of California Water Service Company.

From the very beginning, Elsman initiated several major changes at Cal Water, including the appointment of Peat, Marwick, Mitchell & Co. in November 1939 as the Company's new auditors, replacing Arthur Andersen & Company. It marked the beginning of a relationship with the accounting firm that continues today.

Almost immediately, Elsman made plans to move Cal Water's General Office from San Francisco to San Jose, announcing that space would be provided in the San Jose Water Works building at 374 W. Santa Clara Street. Construction had already begun on a second floor addition to the building, providing for space totaling 7500 sq. ft. to accommodate the Cal Water offices. The Company had been based in San Francisco's Federal Reserve Bank Building for more than a decade. The rented second floor of the San Jose Water Works building would accommodate Cal Water's headquarters for the next 24 years. Elsman would announce that the move was being made *"in the interest of economy and to obtain the maximum benefit from the knowledge and experience of the personnel of both organizations."*

It was also a convenient move for Elsman, who lived in nearby Los Gatos and would continue as president of San Jose Water Works, also a General Water subsidiary, where he had maintained an office at the San Jose company since 1936.

By the end of 1939, Cal Water announced that it was supplying water service to 85,000 customers in 30 California communities. With the start of the new decade, Elsman recommended to the Board that a definite policy be established regarding the declaration of common stock dividends. A resolution was adopted resolving: *That it be the future policy of this Board, insofar as it is practicable, to consider the declaration of dividends on the common stock of the corporation at regular quarterly intervals, beginning with the month of February 1940.*

How to Double Output

FORBES

May 29, 1920   Published Every Two Weeks B. C. Forbes, Editor   20c the Copy

**Public Root
for This
Executive.
Leader at 35**

**U.S. to Dominate
Oil Industry**

**How to Read
Bank Statements**

What to Forget

**Unique Career
of Cyrus Curtis**

**Which Foreign
Bonds to Buy**

RALPH ELSMAN

Excerpt from *Forbes* magazine's 1920 cover story interview with Ralph Elsman, president of the Kings County Lighting Co., Brooklyn, New York...

"At age 35 he is perhaps the youngest public executive in the country" (as head of the third largest gas company in New York state).

"In 1903 at age 18, he was superintendent of a small plant in Mt. Kisco, N.Y., and paid $60 per month by working an average of 18 hours out of every 24...up at 7 a.m., get out after new business, collect bills, read meters, attend to complaints, set transformers, make minor repairs to the lines, etc. This kept him

busy until about 4 o'clock, when he had to start up the plant, fire the boilers and keep things humming until 8 p.m. Then he went to dinner, after which he rode on horseback from Mt. Kisco down to Chappaqua (N.Y.) — five miles distance — and back, patrolling the line to see that all street-lamps were burning. When he had covered all the territory served by the company and replaced all broken lamps, it was usually close to 11 p.m. Then Elsman went home and worked on reports until 1 or 2 o'clock in the morning before turning in for his five or six hours sleep......"

"Of all businesses," says Mr. Elsman, "the public utility business is the one that has been least understood. There is only one way to get public opinion on your side in the public utility business: that is by being fair and square and honest with yourself, with your employees and with the public whom you serve.

"The old method of extreme secrecy is a mistake. We have gotten results simply by laying the cards on the table. We have taken the public into our confidence, shown them our books and opened our hearts to the public. We have taken the stand that a public utility is part of the community and the community, a part of the public utility. One is necessary to the other.

"In any growing, progressive community the public utility concerns have not only to keep abreast of the growth, but a little bit ahead. They must be solvent, progressive public servants if they are going to be kept in that position. If the public knows that a utility company is right and just and is doing its best to give service, if the public is taken into the confidence of the company, then the rest is easy. The public will fight for that company just as it will fight for the community. Wrecking the public utility is just the same as wrecking the community: building ceases, property values shrink, and capital tied up in investments is lost. When the people understand that, and know that the utility is fair, there isn't a fair body of people in the world who wouldn't stand back of that utility."

Chapter 15

Moving to San Jose...

B y the spring of 1940, World War II had already begun and the uncertainties regarding America's involvement in a world-wide conflict surfaced across the nation. Cal Water, meanwhile, began planning the General Office move to San Jose some 50 miles away.

During the first week of June 1940, the Company's 35 General Office employees at the bank building in San Francisco began clearing their desks for the move south to the Santa Clara Valley. The "city by the bay" had been headquarters for the Company almost from its beginning. Once settled in the San Jose facilities, Elsman informed shareholders that: *"The new offices are commodious and practical, and the management is finding that the residence of the Company in San Jose is most convenient for our operations."*

The General Office relocation especially pleased an 18-year-old utility worker in the Company's San Mateo District. Jeptha A. Wade, Jr., who would one day follow in his father's footsteps as the Company's chief engineer, offered his recollections of the move to San Jose and his first meeting with Elsman:

"I had graduated from high school at the end of January in 1940 and had gone to work for the Company in San Mateo as an operations maintenance worker. In April, I learned that one of the young men who was working at the San Francisco headquarters at the time did not want to make the move to San Jose, and it created a vacancy. He was replaced as storekeeper by the office boy, and I jumped at the

chance to apply for his job. It would mean that I could get into clean clothes and not have to dig ditches anymore. I would, however, be taking a cut in salary because my expenses increased having to buy a commute ticket every day from my Burlingame home to San Jose. I worked at the bank building in San Francisco for about a month and half before we officially made the move on June 1.

"Once we had moved to San Jose, I had my first encounter with Mr. Elsman. It was after 5 p.m. one work day and most everyone had gone home. Mr. Elsman needed something run off on the mimeograph machine and I couldn't help him because I didn't know how to do it. He then spotted the stores clerk, the same fellow I had replaced in San Francisco. He was on his way out the door to catch the commuter train back to his home in San Francisco. He had a date or something that night and was in a big hurry when Elsman stopped him. He refused Elsman's request to run the mimeograph machine and Elsman fired him on the spot. That's how I got acquainted with Mr. Elsman."

The future Cal Water vice president also recalled that his first company vehicle was a bicycle provided him to run errands while he served as an office boy at the new San Jose headquarters. Wade had enrolled as an engineering major at the California Institute of Technology when he was called into military service. Following World War II, he graduated from the University and rejoined Cal Water to begin his distinguished career spanning 41 years.

With the General Office move to San Jose, plans were also under way to relocate the Company's statewide water quality laboratory to the new headquarters facilities. The water testing facility had been based in the Stockton District at the Station 2 pump house on River Street since the formation of the Company. The laboratory had operated under the direction of Ken Brown, who had been the sanitary engineer in charge of Cal Water's water quality program since its inception in 1927. Brown left the Company in 1945 to form an engineering consulting firm with David Caldwell. The partnership would expand and prosper under the name, Brown and Caldwell, now one of nation's largest and most respected engineering firms.

In 1929, Brown hired an assistant, Primo Villarruz, a promising chemist who was a recent graduate of the University of California at Berkeley and a native of the Philippines. The two worked together in the Cal Water lab for the next 15 years until Brown left to start his engineering firm. But Brown failed in his attempt to persuade his assistant to come work for him in his new venture. Villarruz remained with the Company as a chemist until his retirement in 1966 after 37 years of service. His son, Bennie, also a chemist, worked side by side with his father for many years. Remarkably, when Bennie retired from Company service in 1993, he ended a Cal Water career spanning 50 years!

Statewide billing operations had been centered at two district locations since the Company's formation in the 1920s. The Stockton District had been recognized as the primary billing office, serving the state's northern area where customer concentration was the heaviest. A smaller East Los Angeles operation was responsible for the billing program in the southern area. In 1947, the East Los Angeles billing operations moved to Stockton, where the statewide billing program would be consolidated and operate for the next 25 years.

Dorothy Vierra Shepard was the third local resident to be hired from the San Jose area when the Company moved the General Office from San Francisco. At the time of her employment in February 1941, she was 17 years old, two weeks short of her 18th birthday.

"There weren't many jobs available for young girls at the time," she said, *"so I had to 'fudge' on my age since the rules said you had to be 18 to apply. When the war came along in December of 1941, we*

were required to have a birth certificate and I thought, 'Oh no ...they are going to fire me because I lied about my age....' so I went to see Mr. Keller, my supervisor at the time, and I told him I had a confession to make. And he said, 'That's OK, Dorothy. We had checked with your school and knew you were going to be 18 that month.'"

That behind her, Shepard began a Cal Water career that would span 43 years with a couple of "family interruptions" along the way.

"When I started I made $65 per month, which was the minimum. As I remember, my paycheck was $16.50 per week," Shepard said. *"The highest paid lady at Cal Water at that time was Dorothy Cotting, who was paid $150 per month, and I had thought to myself, 'Oh, if only some day I could make $150 per month.' Evelyn Hancock, who like myself, had gone to Santa Clara High, was the first employee the Company had hired after they had arrived in San Jose, and then Doris Carlson was hired, and then me. I remember Jep Wade, Jr., was the office boy. At one time I was the Company's youngest employee at the General Office, and then, became the oldest by the time I retired. At the end, I was referred to by the young ladies as 'Ma Shep.'*

"When I was hired, we only had one calculator and that was a manually operated Remington, and we had comptometers that also added, subtracted, multiplied and divided, but with no tape.

"The only time I remember Mr. Elsman coming upstairs to the Cal Water offices was at Christmas time. He came up to shake our hands and wish us a Merry Christmas.

"The secretaries who had come down from San Francisco when we moved to San Jose never brought their lunch to work. Every noontime they would put on their gloves, their hats, their coats and walk downtown for lunch regardless of how hot it was. Up in San Francisco, everyone had always 'dressed' for lunch.

"For a time during the war, we were frozen in our jobs so you

72

couldn't quit if you wanted to. At one time I had wanted to go work at Moffett Field to make more money since the Company wouldn't give us raises. But because of the war, I had to stay. What the Company did do, however, was get me another job working on Saturday for a 'co-op' that gave me $10 more per month. Then, when the war ended in 1945, they gave us a big $5 raise...that was per month!

"I remember one day after we had moved over to the new General Office on North First Street, I thought a bunch of us were all going to be fired. We all had agreed to come to work one day fitted out in yellow dresses or skirts, all just for fun — just to be nutty. And then we decided to wade in the beautiful, new reflecting pool at lunch time. Joe Viguier came out and raised a fume with us. He said there was something like chlorine in the water or whatever. He warned us never again to stick even a foot in that water. That's why I get amazed when I see these people today walking in the pool and having duck races and such.

"We had hard times during my era so we really appreciated things as matters progressed for the better and we got more pay. The people at the Company were very loyal, very dedicated to Cal Water. We were like one big happy family. We shared our problems and we had the support of everybody. And we were thankful for our jobs. It wasn't just an individual trait. It was a spirit that prevailed among most all employees — both men and women."

Dorothy Shepard retired from Company service in 1988 as payroll supervisor and resides today in Wenatchee, Washington.

When Cal Water moved its General Office from San Francisco to San Jose in the summer of 1940, local residents were hired to complement the San Francisco office staff which had made the move to the new headquarters in the South Bay. Among the "locals" added during the months following the move included Evelyn Hancock, second from left, the first local resident to be hired; she was followed by Doris Carlson, far right, and then by Dorothy Vierra Shepard, center. Other office staff members shown here on a special luncheon together during the early 1940s are Vera Conway, left, the first woman employee to work on the general ledger, and Gertrude Williams, second from right. Lady employees always wore hats on these occasions.

For 24 years — from 1940 to 1964 — California Water Service rented General Office space in the San Jose Water Works building at 374 West Santa Clara St., San Jose, California. San Jose Water Works, which has since changed its name to San Jose Water Company, still maintains its headquarters in this building. Cal Water's president, Ralph Elsman, occupied an office on the building's first floor, front left corner. Cal Water personnel occupied the entire second floor which totaled 7500 sq. ft. Second floor windows in front were offices of the Cal Water officers.

Chapter 16

"Are you calling me a liar?"

No sooner had the General Office staff settled into its San Jose facilities before Elsman was confronted by employee efforts to unionize the Company. The Depression Decade had ended and the growing prewar economy began to bring higher-paying job opportunities in competition with the lower pay levels being offered at the time in the utility industry. In several Cal Water districts, utility workers voted to unionize under the auspices of the Congress of Industrial Organization (C.I.O.).

In Bakersfield, 17-year-old Ken Dow joined the Company in January 1938, and he remembers to this day the hard times. He had been assigned to the Company's "bull gang," an ignominious reference to the pick-and-shovel crew of 12 men who were responsible for digging ditches and laying pipe.

"Those with the least seniority on the 'bull gang,' including himself," Dow said, *"were assigned to the front of the line where the work was the hardest breaking the asphalt."* By the time the field workers in the Bakersfield District decided to organize in 1941, Dow had been promoted to storekeeper. He was named to the three-member employee negotiating team *because I had some high school, making me better educated than most of my fellow workers.*

"The first notice we had sent to the Company, which indicated our wish to form a union, was ignored. Finally, the National Labor Relations Board told the Company it had to recognize us because a

majority of the workers in the District had made the request. There were 21 of us at the time. The office workers also came aboard once they saw that everyone in the field had signed on. We all knew we were putting our jobs on the line.

"Our employee negotiating team included Carl Stahlecker and Harry Tedrow, two long-time field employees. Carl was chief pump operator at the time. He was an old German who could hardly read or write. But he is the one that really worked to form the Union Council. And he did work hard for the benefits we received. I can't give Carl enough praise. He was ornery, meaner than the devil, and hard to get along with, but he was honest. He became president of the Cal Water Utility Workers Council and would eventually retire from the Company as superintendent of production.

"I was 20 years old in December 1941 and was scared to death as I got ready to meet with the big shots coming down from the General Office in San Jose: Mr. Dodge, Mr. Call and Mr. Jamison. I was made the team's secretary because I was the only one who could take notes for us. We also had a representative from the C.I.O., Mr. Daugherty.

"The first thing Mr. Dodge wanted to see was the list of Bakersfield people who had signed up for the union. In that very same week we started to negotiate at Bakersfield's old El Tejon Hotel, the news came in that the Japanese had bombed Pearl Harbor and we were at war. Mr. Dodge right away didn't want to continue the meeting because of the war, so we all agreed to resume our meeting in January after the holidays. Our negotiations were tough and right away we were calling each other liars and such. At one point Mr. Dodge got so mad he couldn't see straight. We told him of the problems that were going on in the District and how bad the employees were being treated. We said he was wrong because he was getting bad informa-

tion from the District, and I told him, 'Mr. Dodge, that just isn't right.'
He turned and shouted at me, 'Are you calling me a liar?' And I said
'I don't like to, but that's the way it is.' He settled down and we nego-
tiated for the next four days, continuing sometimes all through the
night. We just took naps right in the meeting room and went out to eat.
Mr. Dodge would take us out and buy our breakfast, lunch, dinner and
snacks.

"As we neared the end of the negotiations, I'll never forget it. We
were up on about the fourth floor of the hotel and Mr. Dodge was
looking out the window onto Chester Avenue at the Bakersfield clock
tower, and we were telling him, 'By golly, this pump operator, Guy
Foster, he joined the Company in 1929 and lived in this house owned
by the Company plus he got his wages.' And we didn't think it was fair
that the Company was going to take the house away from him just
because he was joining the union and now he must pay rent. There
was no way, we said, that was fair to him. So that was the sticking
point to signing the first contract.

"Mr. Dodge whirled from the window and shouted 'G_ _ D_ _ _
it! You're not getting anything more and we're getting out of here, and
you can go on strike or whatever you want to. You can go to hell!'

"It scared the heck out of me. I felt like I was two inches tall. Oh
God, he was mad. He really put on a show. At that moment Carl and
Harry about fell through their chairs. The only guy that wasn't both-
ered by Dodge's outburst was our union negotiator, Mr. Daugherty. It
didn't seem to concern him a bit. He would say in a calm, but loud
voice, 'Go ahead, Mr. Dodge, we can take everything you can throw
at us. We will take care of these guys and you will be out, not these
guys.'

"And that's just the way he talked. Then Mr. Dodge said, 'Well,
maybe we better take a recess.'

77

"We ended up with a two-year contract with raises for all the employees and went on a monthly payroll. I went from $95 dollars to $120 per month as storekeeper. The pump operators went up to $130 from $100. Carl, as the chief pump operator, got a $25 raise to $135 per month. Plus we got vacations and sick leave, which we didn't get before. Only salaried employees and the manager's secretary had been given vacations prior to that time. In the prior three years I had worked for the Company, I never received a vacation. After the contract, I started to get two weeks per year. Mr. Dodge, who was hard but fair, ended up firing the district manager.

"Many years later Mr. Dodge would commend me for standing up to him at the time. He would call me 'Boy.' 'Boy, I am proud of you. I hated you at one time. But I am proud of you now. You are a number one kid.' That was when I had rejoined the Company after coming out of the Navy. Mr. Dodge's word was his bond. He was a straight shooter. Our Bakersfield District was the first to have a union contract, although East Los Angeles had started to organize before we did. They copied our contract and they eventually got the same thing. It was now easier for them to get one signed, and it was Mr. Dodge's old district, too, where he had served as manager in the twenties. The other districts started to come on line with the union, and the Council was formed while I was away during the war."

Dow ended his 47 years of Company service in 1985, retiring as Cal Water's district manager in Visalia.

By the end of 1942, eight districts — Bakersfield, San Mateo, South San Francisco, San Carlos, Bear Gulch, Stockton, East Los Angeles and Contra Costa — had become members of the Utility Workers Union under the auspices of the C.I.O.

The Board of Directors had met two years earlier to authorize payment of the Company's annual pensions totaling $885 per month for the coming year to pay to the following 17 retired employees:

Marcella Quimby	$ 50	W. A. Mott	$ 25
E. C. Wilson	$ 50	A. A. Patton	$ 50
Oscar Mullin	$ 50	George Arnold	$ 50
H. M. Johns	$ 50	William Deicke	$ 50
Kathryn Verkuyl	$ 50	J. H. Moore	$ 50
Fred D. Ellsworth	$100	Eli Oren	$ 50
Perry Hanratty	$ 35	Alfred Pierce	$ 50
C. J. Norman	$ 50	William H. Wolfe	$ 50
Edward Stenhauer	$ 75		

Bakersfield District employees ready the Company entry in the City's 1930s Western Days Parade. Carl Stahlecker, shown in foreground, served early in his career as president of the Company's Utility Workers Union Council and retired as District Superintendent of Production.

Chapter 17

Responding to the national emergency...

Throughout the months preceding the start of U.S. involvement in the war on Dec. 7, 1941, the Company had experienced accelerated growth statewide. It was the result of conditions relating to national defense and the threat of hostilities. Some 5,662 new customers were added during the year, with more than $1 million allocated for plant maintenance and expansion.

Prior to ceasing operations in the Redding District in August of 1941, the Company's Contra Costa District had lost its Martinez service area as a wholesale customer because its citizens approved a bond enabling the community to develop its own source of water. The Martinez action began a series of governmental attempts during the next 20 years to reduce Cal Water's presence in Contra Costa County. The continuing assault on Cal Water's Contra Costa systems would result in the decision to sell the District in 1961.

In the four years following the outbreak of the war, operations of the Company were substantially affected by the national emergency. Many restrictions were placed on the use of materials, resulting in limitations on general construction and maintenance programs. The Company announced that it was cooperating fully with all governmental agencies, including the Office of Civilian Defense, *"to safeguard and protect its water supplies."* At the outbreak of the war, Cal Water purchased War Risk and Bombardment Insurance on its properties.

Among management changes during 1941, Earl C. Elliott retired as chairman of the Board along with Vice President E. B. Walthall, a member of the original Fresno City Water team. Dean Witter, one of the early members of the Cal Water Board, resigned after nine years of service. During his tenure on the Board, approximately $12,596,000 in security sales on behalf of Cal Water had been executed through Dean Witter & Company.

After 15 years honing his executive skills, first under Earl Elliott and Christopher Chenery, and then as the right hand of Ralph Elsman, Fred Dodge and his mettle would be officially recognized in 1942. He was named vice president to complement his existing position as assistant general manager and the Company's official "second in command." Dodge would continue as Elsman's right hand for the next two decades, assuming almost complete control of Cal Water's operations, first as vice president and later as president. He enjoyed, but did not abuse, Elsman's complete confidence.

Dodge had been raised in the Los Angeles area where his father was a farmer, a lifestyle that the elder Dodge would soon recognize was not the calling for his aggressive son. Young Dodge would rather earn his way amid the excitement of the Hollywood night life. He played the drums in a dance band that performed at all the "hot spots" throughout Hollywood, Beverly Hills and Los Angeles, including many of the mansions of the area. By the time Dodge was 23, however, he chose to enter the more sedate life of the business world. In 1923, he went to work for the Janss Brothers, a major land company that was one of the early developers of the Greater Los Angeles area. He was named to manage the firm's Belvedere Water Corporation, which had been formed by the Janss operation to provide water service to its new residential development in the East Los Angeles area. Four years later, the Belvedere Company was acquired by

Federal Water Service Company, and Dodge, who was retained by Federal Water as its local manager, began his 57-year career with California Water Service Company.

In 1942, Cal Water's wartime "Resident Representatives" (today referred to as District or Local Managers) were identified as:

Atherton, Menlo Park, Woodside .... R. E. Terwilliger
Bakersfield .... A. L. Trowbridge
Chico .... W. M. Keach
Contra Costa .... N. C. Nutting
    (Concord, Crockett, Danville, Valona, Port Costa,
    Martinez, Port Chicago, Walnut Creek)
Dixon .... O. C. Dunn
East Los Angeles .... L. L. Camy
Hanford and Visalia .... A. C. Stolp
Hermosa Beach, Redondo Beach .... C. G. Parbury
Livermore .... J. C. Langlois
Lomita Park .... H. N. Hayden
Los Altos .... T. D. Kirkes
Marysville .... P. J. Mathisen
Oroville .... C. L. Nelson
Petaluma .... D. A. Hendrix
San Carlos .... S. R. Kirkes
San Mateo .... A. L. Stolp
South San Francisco .... S. H. Volonte
Stockton .... Frank Suters
Willows .... C. M. Fortner

As the world conflict continued through its first full year, the realities of the potential dangers and the hardships to be encountered gradually emerged. Plans were developed to protect the Company's supply and distribution facilities and guard against service interruptions in case of enemy attack. Windows and buildings were "blacked out" for use as Company control centers, and practice alerts were held to test defense plans. In compliance with orders from the War Production Board, the Company was required to conserve materials and restrict construction expenditures to $551,948 from an original budget of $1,173,804. The difficulties were compounded by the loss of 194 regular employees, 30 of whom had been called to military service. Replacements were made where possible and duties rearranged to avoid interrupts in service. However, new directives from the War Manpower Commission and amendments to the Selective Service Act (authorizing the drafting of personnel for military service) signaled even further difficulties as the war continued.

To help alleviate labor concerns, Cal Water announced to employees in 1943 that it was adopting a wartime emergency policy: *"...permitting any employee (except those who do not get extra compensation for overtime) to forego his or her vacation and to receive extra pay at straight time rates in lieu of the vacation. The choice lay entirely with each individual employee who is entitled to a vacation. In order to make this opportunity available to the employees, it was necessary to obtain advanced approval from the War Labor Board and the Stabilization Unit of the U.S. Treasury Dept."*

Despite these and other offsetting measures, replacements had to be found for 144 more regular employees in 1943. The high turnover resulted not only from the increased demand from the military, but also from the growing competition in the job market fueled by the wartime economy. As 1943 came to a close, the Company rolls totaled 257 regular employees and 31 temporary workers meeting the needs of 97,613 customers. Despite the war conditions, Company growth continued unabated with 17,780 new customers added during the five-year period ending on Dec. 31, 1943. While customer growth remained strong and the problems of wartime continued, municipal takeover attempts would plague Company districts.

In March of 1943, Bakersfield officials sought citizen approval of a ballot measure authorizing the acquisition of the water company. The proposal was defeated in a city-wide vote by a 2 to 1 margin. Within a year, the City of Chico would also be considering a feasibility plan for municipal acquisition of its electric, gas and water utilities.

By the summer of 1944, two and a half years into the war, Company customers had grown increasingly apprehensive over a possible enemy attack on the nation's home soil. On one occasion in the Chico District, the wife of the City's most prominent physician called the local Cal Water office, suggesting the water tanks be camouflaged. She expressed genuine concern that the supply would be threatened if the water tanks became enemy targets during an air attack. The local manager reassured her that every possible precaution was being taken to protect the City's water supply.

But among the home front's many programs and supporting activities in behalf of the war effort, none would be embraced more enthusiastically than the phenomenon known as the Victory Gardens. Millions of homeowners across the nation participated in planting backyard fruits and vegetables to supplement the nation's food supply. A Company-wide survey indicated that 80 percent of Cal Water families had become urban farmers by establishing gardens in support of the war effort. As 1944 was ending, a notice appeared in the Company's employee newsletter from the U.S. Government's War Department urging victory gardeners to maintain their vegetable production in 1945. Major General Edmund P. Gregory, the U.S. Quartermaster General, wrote Cal Water employees:

"Your victory gardens together with those throughout the country, are credited with producing 40 percent of the fresh vegetables grown in the United States during 1944. This has been a most worthy accomplishment — so worthy, that we are asking victory gardeners this year to repeat their performance of 1944. In fact," he wrote, *"with the least favorable food outlook and the added need for military supply, we are hoping that you will surpass your record of the past season."*

The government's plea to Cal Water for support noted that vegetables grown in the nation's victory gardens and used to supplement the home's food supply:

"...had made available larger quantities of commercially canned vegetables for the Armed Forces. According to the government's assessment, additional hardship would have occurred at home if victory gardens had not contributed so liberally to the nation's food supply."

The Company also was awarding Victory Garden credits to customers that resulted in lower water rates for participating homeowners.

Fortunately, governmental restrictions on materials and construction were relaxed during 1944, thus enabling the Company to enlarge and improve plant facilities. But employee turnover continued to run high, reaching 43 percent for the year. Sixty-five employees were now serving in the military and 99 regular workers had chosen to seek other employment.

By the summer of 1944, many of Cal Water's employees were on duty throughout the world as the war continued into its third year. Partial lists of service personnel were noted in the Company's newsletters:

George Stevenson	Richard Clendenin
Nat Kendall	Gary Schaub
Vernon Gomez	John Sward
Vernon Ruedy	George Singer
Bill Lewis	Russell Frank
John Lockhart	Jack Call
Donald Camper	William Doherty
John Broyles	Ceasar Pardini
Albert Jacobson	Troy Anderson
Harold Palmer	James McGoyne
Clarence Murschel	Carl Scimeca
William Dolan, Jr.	Joseph Cardoza
Roy Rector	Marie Minners
Joseph Galli	Al Poulter
Doris Hefner	William Nahmens
Jeptha A. Wade, Jr.	Ken Dow
Wes Webber	Dorothy Codding
Reed Surber	Tom Dowd
Wayne Ladd	

Officers, General Office managers and a few special guests attended this Christmas holiday party in December of 1943 at the Company's "River House" printing facility, adjacent to the General Office at 374 W. Santa Clara St., San Jose. Party participants were, from left, "Jamie" Jamison, Harry Keller, Swede Duchene, Evan Green, Monty Hawks, Howard Wenrich, Ken Brown, George Williams, Ed Beall, Bucky Harris, Fred Trees, Jack Rossum, Ben Skillings, Fred Dodge, Carl Mau, Harlan Hulick, Primo Villarruz, Vern Lynn, Ernie Shannon, Karl Sundin, Louis Huff, Ralph Shupe, Jack Kelley, Al Poulter, Pete Palma, Earl Elliott, Jr. and John Ford. Ken Brown, in white coat at left, was a Cal Water sanitary engineer for 16 years before leaving to form the engineering firm of Brown and Caldwell.

Former longtime Visalia leadership...Clayton Rookard, left, office manager, and Ken Dow, district manager, who joined the Company in 1938 at age 17. As a member of the Bakersfield District in 1941, Dow served on the District's three-member employee negotiating team which won Company acceptance of the utility workers' first union contract.

The Company's Bear Gulch reservoir in Atherton provides District customers with a supplemental surface water supply from the area's watershed.

It's Marian Broughton's birthday and time for another GO luncheon celebration back in May of 1944. Enjoying the festivities were, seated, from left, Gertrude Williams, Anita Rohlfing, Betty DeMeza, Dorothy Vierra Shepard, Harriet Descalzo, Evelyn Hancock, Miriam Eckstrand, Thelma Osgood and the honoree, Marian Broughton. Standing, from left, Ann Kennard, Genevieve Smith, Marge Valente, Doris Carlson, Margaret Gleason, Vera Conway, Louise Grabow and Jewel Hughes.

Chapter 18

"Keep them busy while I find the money..."

Without question, 1945 would herald the beginning of a dynamic new era for California Water Service Company. From its very beginning in 1926, the Company had been held captive by the eastern holding companies and their financial interests. The yoke was finally broken on March 29, 1945, propelling the utility into uncharted terrain as a company now owned by the public, preparing to meet the explosive growth of the post-war years. Ralph Elsman announced to the Board that General Water, Gas and Electric Co. had sold its entire holdings in the Company of 116,568 shares to the following investment bankers:

Union Securities Corp. .... 34,797 shares
Harriman Ripley & Co., Inc. .... 20,877 shares
W. C. Langley & Co. .... 17,398 shares
Hornblower & Weeks .... 8,699 shares
Kuhn, Loeb & Co. .... 34,797 shares

On May 11, 1945, the investment houses made a public offering of all Company-held stock at $39 per share. The sale of stock brought wide distribution of ownership to shareholders in 38 states. To its owners of 139,000 shares of preferred stock, the Company provided the option of either exchanging their shares for a new preferred offering or redeeming the stock for $26.25 per share plus accrued dividends. The Company also acquired more working capital later in the year by selling 27,780 shares of additional common stock at $30 per share.

The saga behind the Company's venture into the realm of public ownership could not have been realized but for the reputation, courage and business acumen of Cal Water's 60-year-old president and chief executive, Ralph Elsman.

General Water was the owner of both San Jose Water Works and California Water Service Company, with Elsman serving in the dual role as the chief executive for the two companies. In the months prior to the public offering, a financial group, which could be described today as corporate raiders, had gained control of General Water and its assets. Reportedly, the group's plan was to sell off the various properties of California Water Service Company to underlying municipalities and make a tidy profit as the Company was gradually reduced to nothing. Elsman became aware of the scheme and set into motion his own plan to gain control of both San Jose Water Works and California Water Service Company.

The raiders notified Elsman of their plans to visit Palm Springs with their families early in 1945, expressing interest in taking time to inspect their California properties. The hidden agenda, of course, was to determine the value and marketability of the West Coast assets. Elsman dispatched his vice president and right arm, Fred Dodge, to Palm Springs to arrange vacation accommodations for the families and to greet the visitors upon their arrival. Using a chartered plane, Dodge had been instructed by Elsman to escort his guests around the state to acquaint them with the Cal Water properties.

"Show them everything and keep them busy as long as you can, while I find the money," were Elsman's instructions to Dodge. He explained that he would need enough time to travel East and persuade his banking contacts to loan him the funds to purchase all outstanding stock of both California Water Service Company and San Jose Water Works. His 40-year, impeccable reputation within both the utility industry and the financial community had preceded him. The Mellons of Pittsburgh, together with some major New York banks, rallied to his aid. With Elsman's personal assets pledged as collateral, including his Los Gatos home and other properties, the banks agreed to provide him a personal loan to strike a deal for the two California companies. Before returning to California, Elsman had also met with the investment bankers who agreed to be the third party in the deal, allowing for repayment of Elsman's personal bank loans through funds generated by the public offering.

Dodge, in the meantime, had been doing his job well, escorting his guests from one well site to another, then to the water tanks, in his attempt to be thorough (and waste some time). But his best efforts at consuming time would come through the cooperation of the U.S. Army Air Corps.

The country was still months away from declaring victory in both Europe and Asia, and thus continued in a high state of national alert. Unfortunately for the pilot of the chartered plane carrying Dodge and his visitors, he mistakenly flew over a restricted military area, resulting in the arrival of a menacing fighter escort. The errant aircraft was forced to land at a nearby military airfield, much to Dodge's delight, and the group was detained for the next several days before a security clearance could be obtained.

By the time they had arrived back in Palm Springs, Elsman was waiting. Over the the next two days he successfully negotiated with his adversaries, offering cash for their entire stock holdings in the two companies. Within several months, California Water Service Company and San Jose Water Works were under full public ownership with Elsman in total command of both companies.

Following the public offering, discussions had been held between Ralph Elsman and Cal Water's McCutchen attorney, Robert

Minge Brown, regarding the feasibility of merging the two public companies; however, there had been indications that the City of San Jose might attempt to acquire San Jose Water Works. If condemnation proceedings moved forward, it would place a premium on the San Jose Water Works stock, affording a possible tax advantage to the San Jose shareholders. No action was taken, reportedly, because of difficulty in arriving at a valuation for the two firms that would be acceptable to the California Public Utilities Commission. The merger idea would be revisited by Elsman and Brown in later years.

Chapter 19

"Well, go find some customers so we can get started..."

With the ending of the war in August of 1945 and the independence of the Company secured, Cal Water's future seemed bright. However, despite the promising outlook, Cal Water's future would remain difficult and uncertain for almost another two decades.

Its financial condition had been weakened when it became a public company, and the war had depleted its experienced staff. The need was especially critical for professional engineers, whose skills were required to meet the post-war building boom that was already underway by the end of 1945.

The new public company was further burdened by the immediate demand to strengthen its systems where maintenance and supplies had been curtailed by the restrictions imposed during four years of war. Faced with the continuing threat of municipal ownership actions, upgrading and maintenance became a major priority. By the end of the year, customer totals had already reached 105,110 and another city, San Carlos, had announced that it was continuing its discussion on the feasibility of acquiring the Company's local water system.

Aware of Cal Water's many adversities and challenges, Elsman and Dodge would painstakingly address the critical needs of the post-war era. The Company was about to enter a period that would provide the greatest sustained growth since its founding. From Jan. 1, 1946, to Dec. 31, 1957, Cal Water gained an average of more than 10,500 new customers per year, and by 1958 the customer base would total 231,845.

Joining the new hires would be former employees who had been discharged from military service. Among those returning to the General Office was Jack Call, the Company's former Petaluma manager who had served in the African campaign and had been awarded the Bronze Star, rising in rank from private to lieutenant colonel with the 15th Air Force. He became purchasing agent for the Company and later served as head of personnel and corporate secretary before retiring in 1959.

The professional staff would grow as young engineering graduates were hired, including future assistant chief engineers Parker Robinson, Jack Prendergast and Dave Heninger, who would later retire as chief engineer. Jack Rossum was selected to head the laboratory as sanitary engineer, replacing Ken Brown.

Twenty-four-year-old Robinson joined Cal Water in 1946 following three years of military service as an Army officer during the European campaign. He recalls those early days at the Company immediately following World War II:

"Cal Water operated almost totally from the second floor of the San Jose Water Works building, except for our laboratory, which was downstairs in a separate building out back. The second floor accommodated Cal Water's engineering, accounting, purchasing, executives, stores, personnel...the whole operation. We didn't have air conditioning then, and in the summer time when it got hot, it was miserable up on that second floor. In 1946, there were fewer than 50 people working at GO. There were maybe eight of us working in engineering, which included our teenage secretary, Phyllis Massey, who became Phyllis Lovoi and retired from Cal Water in 1991. Even though San Jose Water and Cal Water were in the same building (and Elsman was the head of both companies), our operations were completely separate and we had very little contact with one another. We

performed the lab work for San Jose, but that was it. We didn't even know the people from San Jose. Our billing office, of course, was still over in Stockton where it had been located since the start of the Company. When I first came to work, the engineers made up the annual budget without going into the districts to discover first hand what was needed. I took over operations and maintenance in the late forties and became responsible for the budget. I wanted to get a better feel for things out in the districts...what was needed — where, how, why. That's when we started to tour every district each summer. Not too long afterward, the construction people also thought it would be a good idea. The construction budget tour started after we had started our tours. Fifty years later, the tours are still in place."

Former Cal Water office boy, Jeptha A. Wade, Jr., rejoined the Company in 1947 after completing military service and receiving his engineering degree from Cal Tech. Once the professional staff at General Office had been sufficiently augmented, Elsman took steps to strengthen the Company's precarious financial position. George Williams, a retired financial expert from General Electric and Elsman's neighbor in Los Gatos, was hired to begin work on a program to increase Company water rates. Incredibly, residential rates had never been raised in any district throughout the state since the Company's founding in 1926!

Williams began working with Robert Minge Brown, the Company attorney from the McCutchen firm, in the effort to win approval of the State's Public Utilities Commission to raise water rates in three company districts — Dixon, Willows and Petaluma. The two men were, in effect, pioneering the development of the rate-making process for the Company, and to a great degree, for private water utilities in California.

Cal Water's first public hearing for a district rate increase was an unforgettable occasion for Robert Minge Brown. The year was 1947 and Brown, accompanied by Williams, was scheduled to appear before a judge from the Public Utilities Commission in the small town of Dixon. The public hearing was scheduled for the town hall at 10 a.m. on a weekday morning. The Dixon water rates had not been changed since established by the predecessor company in 1915. The Company was seeking a 25-cent increase in the existing one dollar monthly surcharge and a minimal increase in the quantity rate.

To the dismay of the PUC presiding judge, there were no citizens in sight as the proceedings were about to begin in the town's council chambers at the appointed hour. The judge had just traveled 65 miles from San Francisco together with a full entourage of Commission staff.

"Where are the customers?" the judge impatiently asked Brown, who in turn explained that notices of the meeting had been mailed to all local citizens in a proper and timely manner. *"Well, go find some customers so we can get this thing started,"* demanded the jurist.

As he recalled the event years later, Cal Water's future chairman said he left the town hall, somewhat perplexed over his unusual assignment. He proceeded to approach Dixon citizens walking along downtown Main Street, using his considerable powers of persuasion to win cooperation from reluctant town folk to attend the hearing. With a group of local citizens in tow, Brown returned to the town hall and the appeased judge called the hearing to order.

In addition to Dixon that year, Cal Water applied for rate increases in Willows and Petaluma, which were finally approved in 1949. The increases brought an additional $72,000 in annual gross revenue, a welcome new source of funds for the cash-strapped Company. The following year, rate increases were sought in six more districts — Hanford, Visalia, Bakersfield, Oroville, Livermore and

South San Francisco, requesting a total of $252,600 in added revenue.

In an effort to further shore up its tenuous post-war financial condition, the Company sold 15,652 additional shares of common stock in November of 1947, thus increasing the total number of common shares outstanding to 210,000. Existing first-mortgage bond debt was also increased to $12,782,000 following the sale of the $ 1.5 million issue.

In August of 1946, the Company acquired the water facilities in a new residential community known as Broadmoor with 215 customers. It was predicted that the new development, located near South San Francisco, would increase to 550 customers when completed.

Earlier that year, Fred Dodge assumed the duties as general manager of the Company, a title previously held by the president, Ralph Elsman.

Fred L. Dodge
President - 1956-1965
Truly a Company icon, he joined
California Water Service Company during
its formation years of the 1920s as
manager of the East Los Angeles District.
His remarkable career with the Company
would span 57 years.

The late 1940s...Cal Water's accounting, purchasing and stores personnel in GO facilities on the second floor of the San Jose Water Works building...the Company's headquarters for 24 years! The gentlemen standing in the rear, from left, are Frank Shotts, stores accountant; Ralph Shupe, assistant secretary and assistant treasurer; Harlan Hulick, vice president and treasurer; and to his left, standing at the window, are Dorothy Shepard and Ann Kennard. Seated at desks, left row from rear to front are Gert Williams, Wanda Starnes, Jenny Kelley, Jean Washkuhn and Leslie Armstrong. Seated at desks next to window, from rear to front, Evelyn Hamrick, Marjorie West, Jane Rowley, Margaret Andrews and Betty DeMeza. Karl Sundin, another staff member, was on vacation.

Parker Robinson
He would be among the new engineers joining the Company following World War II, then later taking a leadership role in computerizing the engineering department and district operations.

George L. Williams
*Company vice president
who helped pioneer Cal
Water's rate-making process
during the late 1940s.*

Jack Call
*A former chief clerk in the Petaluma
District, Call returned from World
War II service to help the Company
meet the dramatic challenges of the
post-war boom as personnel director
and corporate secretary.*

*In 1945, San Francisco Peninsula employees and families enjoyed a venison
barbecue as guests of Bob Terwilliger, Bear Gulch superintendent (center
wearing cook's hat). The event had been an annual event hosted by Bob for
some 25 years. At top left, standing, is guest Fred Dodge, Cal Water vice
president (and future president). Also shown are LaDreu and Vertalyne Stolp,
second row, seated in front. LaDreu was manager of the Peninsula District.*

Chapter 20

The first steps toward industry leadership...

With its new independence as a publicly held water utility, Cal
Water became active in state and regional water issues primarily as
they affected the well-being of the Company's operating districts.
This leadership role in the industry has prevailed through the years,
continuing to the present day. Its genesis most probably can be identified with the work of Cal Water's Vice President Carl F. Mau, who
represented the Company on public relations matters. Trained as an
engineer, Mau had been on the staff of the California Public Utilities
Commission.

In 1946, Mau was sent to Los Angeles by Elsman to locate a
supplemental water source to the Company's groundwater supply in
the Hermosa-Redondo District, which was located near the ocean.
Governmental studies had shown that excessive groundwater pumping in the area was pulling seawater into the mainland, destroying
water wells as a result of salt-water intrusion.

Mau succeeded in organizing what today is known as the West
Basin Water Association, a group of cities, water companies and large
water users in the area who were affected by the underground seawater problem. These included the oil refineries of the area and companies that had been formed to support the war effort. Assisting him was
the San Jose public relations firm of Russell Pierce and Co. and
consultant Harry Kerr, who would one day become Cal Water's vice
president of public affairs. Cal Water, together with the City of Tor-

rance and the Palos Verdes Water Company, had filed a lawsuit against the groundwater users of the area as a means to protect and identify their water rights through a process known as adjudication.

The action also was intended to freeze the rights of all producers who had increased their pumping since the beginning of World War II. It sought to prevent them from establishing water rights adversely to the Company and others who had withdrawn water from the Basin for many years. The lawsuit, with its various reports and studies, took 15 years to be resolved, but finally established individual water rights based upon a history of prior use.

By the time of the settlement, however, water rights were not as critical, since the long adjudication process had convinced surrounding communities that supplemental water was a dire need for the area.

The citizens voted to establish the West Basin Municipal Water District, which was given authorization to pay back taxes, thus enabling annexation to the Metropolitan Water District of Southern California and the purchase of surface water from its Colorado River source.

After Mau retired in 1960, Jeptha A. Wade, Jr., assumed Mau's responsibilities, undertaking a similar action in behalf of Cal Water in Los Angeles County's Central Basin, the location of the Company's East Los Angeles service area. Using the West Basin plan as a guide, Wade filed an adjudication action known as Cal Water vs. Compton to establish water rights for users in the Central Basin Municipal Water District. Once again, the action would bring an additional water supply from the Metropolitan Water District to the area's water utilities and other users, including the Company's East Los Angeles District.

Chapter 21

"...72 years of age and could no longer properly perform his duties...."

In retrospect, the decade of the fifties had begun on a positive note for California Water Service Company with the hiring of a 25-year-old graduate of the University of California at Berkeley. He was given duty as an operations maintenance worker in the San Mateo District, thus beginning the 50-year Company career for C. H. "Bud" Stump, culminating in his leadership role as president, chairman, chief executive officer and director.

The decade, however, had mixed blessings for the fortunes of California Water Service Company. On one hand, its phenomenal internal annual growth rate has never been duplicated. Yet, it was also an era of uncertainty with a strike of the Company utility workers looming in 1950, primarily over retirement and welfare benefits. The Company was also engaged with city after city in their continuing efforts to confiscate its utility operations. Ironically, the constant governmental assault on the Company's water systems eventually proved a blessing in disguise with future sales of district operations playing an important role in the Company's continuing quest for financial stability.

Before 1950, Cal Water did not have in place a standardized pension program, with retirement compensation coming only after an official decree from the Board of Directors as noted in the Board minutes of the January 1946 meeting, reading in part:

"The president then informed the Board of the desirability of

retiring from active service Mr. Edmund S. J. Baldwin, bookkeeper at the Bakersfield office. He stated that Mr. Baldwin, (an original employee) employed by the Company for twenty years, was 72 years of age and could no longer properly perform his duties because of ill health. Upon motion duly made and seconded, the following resolution was unanimously adopted:

'Resolve that the payment of the sum of fifty-eight dollars and 33/100 per month to Mr. Edmund S. J. Baldwin upon his retirement from active service, effective April l, 1946, be....hereby authorized and approved; providing, however, that nothing herein contained shall be construed as creating or recognizing any obligation whatsoever on the part of this corporation to continue such payment of fifty-eight dollars and 33/100 per month for any period whatsoever, it being understood that either this Board of Directors or the officers of this corporation may adjust the amount of such monthly payment or terminate or discontinue the same at any time.'"

In 1950, the Company anticipated a strike by members of the utility union as disagreements arose over pension and welfare benefits. Heated negotiations dragged on and the animosity between employees and management grew with each passing day. Finally an agreement was reached and the strike avoided.

The main thrust of the contract called for improvements in the Company's pension and welfare programs, which were to be funded partially through employee contributions. Retirement would bring a monthly payment of $125 at age 65 after a minimum of 25 years of service. This would include Social Security benefits. Participating employees would contribute two cents per hour and the Company would contribute six cents per hour to the retirement fund. Officers were not eligible to participate and had no retirement program in effect.

The welfare plan included both disability and life insurance, in addition to a health plan to cover medical and surgical care. Participating employees contributed one percent of earnings up to $3,000 per year, replacing the contribution previously made to the state for disability insurance, with the Company paying the balance of the coverage. Once again, officers did not participate in the plan.

The pension and medical benefits awarded in 1950 were minuscule when compared to those of the present day. But the agreement was a major breakthrough in establishing a pension and medical program that was officially sponsored by the Company.

Dressing for work...

"I had walked into the Cal Water office in August of 1954 to answer an employment ad just wearing a little pink dress and sandals. I really hadn't planned on being interviewed that day. I thought I would just go down and put in my name and that would be it, and if they decided they wanted to interview me, they would call. But as it turned out, Joe Viguier, the personnel manager, interviewed me right then and there. When I arrived back home my mother said the president's secretary, Mrs. Nuernberg, had called and left a message. 'Would you tell her that she has the job, but would you please tell her to wear hose when she reports to work?' In the 50s, you always wore hose (that's silk stockings)."

Bobbie Nelson, retired, 1991; 37 years service; Cal Water's first woman officer; asst. corp. secretary/head of personnel

Chapter 22

Troubling times amidst
the post-war boom...

Personal tragedy befell Ralph Elsman during the 1950s, while the Company itself was undergoing difficult times as the threat of municipal ownership intensified.

In 1950, his eldest child, Ralph, Jr., was reported missing in action while serving as gunner aboard a B-29 during the Korean War. He would be declared dead after seven years. The loss of his son was a devastating blow for Elsman, and both family and co-workers observed that he never again was the same person. Then, in 1957, he and his wife suffered another family loss when their oldest daughter, Mary Louise, died at age 29 from complications resulting from what was thought to be just a minor illness. She left a husband and their five children, who were all under the age of five. During this period, Elsman was making four to five trips annually down to the Central San Joaquin Valley to visit his second son, Dick, who was mentally handicapped and under treatment in the state hospital in Porterville.

Throughout this time of personal suffering, Elsman would endure the mounting pressures of public ownership activity while striving to maintain the Company's financial integrity and high standard of operations.

Earthquakes had hit southern California during July and August of 1952, causing an estimated $100 million in widespread damage. Fortunately, only the Company's Bakersfield District was affected, with damage to the water system amounting to approximately

$35,000. Water service to customers remained uninterrupted, despite the fact that buildings within the City of Bakersfield had been struck severely. It was the same year Vernon Lynn had taken over as chief engineer of the Company, a position he would hold for the next 14 years. His tenure in that post would be the second longest in Company history.

Throughout the 1950s, Elsman authorized the sale of four Company service areas — Lomita Park, Hanford, Petaluma and Contra Costa, providing service to 32,400 total customers. The communities had all sought to own and operate their water systems and Elsman was in no mood to do battle to retain ownership. In most cases, extensive maintenance and repair were required and the Company's current financial resources did not permit the necessary renovations.

In 1951, a portion of the Contra Costa District was the Company's first casualty of the decade when the 1,437 residents of the Gregory Garden area of Pleasant Hill voted to construct their own water system through passage of an $800,000 bond issue. The community was aided by a grant from the National Production Authority. This was followed in 1952 by the loss of Walnut Creek as a wholesale customer. The City had voted to join the East Bay Municipal Water District and receive its supply from the District's sources. Then, in January of 1957, Cal Water negotiated a $1.9 million sale of its water system to the City of Hanford in the San Joaquin Valley.

Two years later, there was further erosion of the Company's Contra Costa District when a citizens group formed the San Ramon County Water District. Through a negotiated sale with the water district, Cal Water sold a portion of its service area, which included communities along the San Ramon Valley corridor, to the Town of Danville. That same year, also through mutual agreement, the Company sold its Petaluma District to the City. Both transactions that year brought a total cash infusion of approximately $4.5 million.

In the meantime, Cal Water was in discussions with the County water district for the sale of the Company's last and largest service area in Contra Costa. Voters had created an improvement district within the water district, authorizing a bond issue to purchase the Company's remaining properties in the area. It was agreed that for $13.4 million, the water agency would take ownership of the Company's Concord water system and other nearby service areas, including the community of Pleasant Hill. The transfer took place on Feb. 17, 1961, ending several years of Contra Costa County Water District's aggressive pursuit for ownership of the Cal Water system.

The long and disappointing saga of the Company's efforts to serve and properly maintain its Contra Costa service area is best told by Jeptha A. Wade, Jr., who at the time was a member of the Company's executive staff.

"It was a shame that things developed as they did," Wade explained.

"The post-war water development period in Contra Costa happened at a time when we really didn't have the financial strength to keep up. We were growing so rapidly in California during the fifties that every nickel we could get was spent on new construction, and Elsman really didn't feel he could raise enough money necessary to rebuild the Contra Costa system.

"The water network we had developed for the Contra Costa area with the Chenery Reservoir during the early thirties had been sufficient up until the time the post-war period hit. Residents from the East Bay began to come over the hill looking for country living in Contra Costa County, within an easy commute to the Bay Area.

"Suddenly the County had this tremendous boom. At one point in the early fifties, we were adding 10,000 customers per year to our system in Contra Costa alone. The population explosion was a huge strain, compounded by the fact that there still remained great material

shortages from the war.

"During the thirties, Cal Water had used cast iron pipe as its basic standard for construction; but the pipe was not available after the war, at least in the quantity that we needed for Contra Costa. Some things, however, were in plentiful supply, including copper pipe and brass fittings. But cast iron pipe and even asbestos cement pipe were unavailable. Production facilities just didn't exist for supplying the demand. We would get maybe one carload of pipe per year, so when this very vigorous growth started in Contra Costa, the decision was consciously made that we would try to meet the developers' demand with the only pipe that was available at the time.

"There was a great surplus of pipe used by the army in the invasion of Europe to provide fuel to the front lines for the tanks and other mechanized war equipment. Miles of temporary steel pipelines had been laid during the course of the war and when hostilities ended, there was a vast inventory of four-, six- and eight-inch steel pipe available that had been manufactured out of relatively thin steel during the war.

"It became known as invasion pipe, and following the war, we bought it knowing that the pipe wouldn't last forever. But it was everyone's opinion that the pipe should last 20 years, at which time we would be in a position to replace it. Unfortunately, such would not be the case." Wade explained how one misfortune after another occurred in the effort to keep pace with housing construction, including multiple leaks from the newly installed steel pipe.

"Post-war developers, who were trying to meet the demand for low-cost housing, had decided it wasn't necessary to put in wood flooring. It all could be done, they said, with a concrete slab, and to keep the slab from breaking, they placed a steel mesh in the concrete to provide reinforcement. The water pipes and the plumbing to the water heater and to the furnace had been all laid before the slab was

poured, a situation which would create its own set of future problems. We unknowingly had built a very effective battery that generated electrical currents to the pipe. It was like a blowtorch boring holes in the steel pipe through every imperfection of the coating of the pipe.

"Compounding our dilemma was the developers' decision to simplify matters by making the sidewalk and the curb all one integral piece. As a consequence, the water pipes were installed outside the sidewalk over an area in which the homeowners eventually would plant their shrubs and landscaping.

"Within a few months, we started getting calls to come and fix the leaks. A week later the same customers would call, and the Company's leak crews were again dispatched. Each visit would result in tearing up the customer's landscaping to get to the water pipe."

Bill Lewis, who at the time was the Company's superintendent of the Contra Costa District, vividly recalls the hectic period preceding the sale of the District:

"We were repairing as many as 85 leaks a day with five repair crews and a contractor going around digging them out. A main would blow and you had to fix it. You couldn't wait until morning. As superintendent I was on call 24 hours every day. I was out as many as 10-12 times each night checking leaks."

According to Wade, a series of meetings were finally held among the Company's top executives and estimates indicated there would be a substantial cost in attempting to upgrade the Contra Costa system. *"We took our findings back to Mr. Elsman,"* Wade said, *"explaining what it would take to fix the problem even if we could get the right materials. Elsman told us, frankly, we couldn't raise the money at that time to do what had to be done in upgrading the system. Consequently, the decision was made to face reality and begin plans to relinquish our holdings in Contra Costa."*

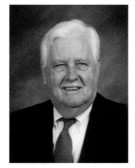

Chesley G. "Fergie" Ferguson
Joined the Company in 1953 and served until 1973, the last 11 years as vice president of rates and regulations. Prior to coming to Cal Water, he was a general staff engineer for 17 years with the California Public Utilities Commission.

Jeptha A. Wade, Jr.
Vice President of California Water Service Company from 1962 to 1987. He first joined the Company in 1940 as an operations maintenance worker in the San Mateo District. After college and World War II service, he rejoined Cal Water full-time in 1947 to begin a 40-year Company career. He served 21 years as chief engineer.

Bill Lewis
Went to work for the Company's East Los Angeles District at age 18 in November 1941 in the billing department at the Whittier Street commercial office. After World War II service and a few other work interruptions along the way, he retired in 1989. During his last 25 years of service, he was purchasing agent at the General Office.

The '52 Bakersfield Quake
When this Company tank toppled, it split open and water gushed out in a huge wave. Despite the fact the City of Bakersfield suffered severe damage as a result of the earthquake, Company loss was limited to approximately $35,000.

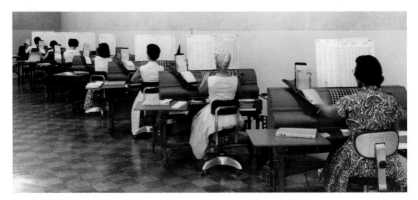

For decades before the advent of the data processing/computer age, the Company's Central Billing Office was located in the Stockton District. In this 1959 photograph, Stockton employees are shown operating the National Cash Register machine in preparation for customer billing. The conversion to electronic billing was completed by December of 1968 after the billing department had moved to San Jose.

Cal Water engineers on tour of the Hanford District during the early 1950s. From left, front row, Bob Corridan, Ray Zimmerman, Harvey Gorman, Mike Calleri, Ken Foy. Back row, from left, Andy Soule, Bruce Folendorf, George Campbell, Dick Menden, Dave Hendrix, Bob Smith, Jeptha Wade, Jr., Hank Hammond.

Chapter 23

Despite the "highs," pessimism would persist...

Cal Water would have lost another major water system during the decade had not Stockton District customers shown their total support for the Company's city operations. The Stockton City Council approached the Company in 1953 regarding the purchase of its water system at a cost to be financed through a city-wide bond election. Elsman inexplicably agreed to negotiate a sales price. However, he did indicate to the City that while the Company had no desire to sell, he would cooperate *"if he was convinced the people of Stockton were in favor of such a move."* Elsman explained the Company's position in a letter sent to all customers, stating that:

"Should the purchase of the Company facilities be approved by the people of Stockton and our price accepted by the city officials, the Company will cooperate in every way possible to facilitate the transfer of the properties." Elsman said the Company would not oppose the City's water bond election and that the important question of city ownership rested entirely with the citizens of Stockton.

On Aug. 25, 1953, Cal Water notified city officials that the sales price was $9,350,000, and the City Council immediately began plans for a bond election in the amount of $11,800,000. Subsequently, on Oct. 13, 1953, Stockton citizens demonstrated wide support for Cal Water by defeating the unopposed bond measure, which would have financed the purchase of the Company's water system. After this vote of confidence by customers, Elsman strongly opposed all future

113

attempts by the City to acquire the water company.

While the fifties were difficult years for Cal Water as it struggled to keep its statewide network intact, there were, nevertheless, positive developments. In addition to being part of the greatest growth period in Company history, the decade brought Cal Water's first major acquisition since 1936. The Company purchased the Suburban Water Company on Jan. 2, 1953. The water system was adjacent to Cal Water's Los Altos District in Santa Clara County and served 5,657 customers. The acquisition increased new services for the year by 9,275 and brought total Company customers to 184,175.

In June of that year, Robert Minge Brown, the McCutchen attorney who had been instrumental in developing the Company's aggressive program for rate increases, was named to the Board of Directors. He replaced retiring E. B. Walthall, who had been a director since 1928 and one of the original members of Cal Water's first executive team. In addition to Elsman and Dodge, who served as inside directors, Brown's fellow Board members included his associate from the McCutchen law firm, A. Crawford Greene, Sr. The Company's remaining directors were San Jose businessmen — Paul L. Davies, Charles M. O'Brien, Fred J. Oehler, E.N. Richmond and attorney R.C. Leib.

As new development continued at an accelerated pace during 1954, the Company received a major decision from the CPUC to ease the financial strain of post-war growth. The Commission's so-called main extension rules were modified, reducing Company cash flow requirements on new construction. California water utilities were allowed to make refunds over a 20-year period on advances developers had made to the utility for the construction cost of new water systems. Previously, the subdivider's total cost was refunded before the development had been fully completed, thus restricting the earnings

114

potential on the Company's investment.

On Jan. 1, 1957, Ralph Elsman rewarded Fred Dodge for his 30 years of loyal service, naming him Cal Water's fourth president since its founding. Elsman continued as chairman and chief executive. And later that same year, a young attorney and CPA from Utah answered a Cal Water advertisement in the Wall Street Journal for an assistant treasurer. Ralph D. Lindberg was hired and ten years later replaced retiring Fred Dodge as president. The new employee recalled the pessimism that prevailed at the time among some of the officers of the Company. They felt the future was in municipal ownership, sensing that the Company would become weaker and weaker as condemnation actions continued. But Lindberg dismissed the negative views.

Neither were there words of gloom expressed by Elsman in his letter to shareholders on Feb. 5, 1957:

"...since assuming the presidency, it has been my privilege to see this Company grow to be the largest privately owned operating water utility in the United States, with its ownership divided among 9,000 shareholders throughout the nation....The Company is happy to have played an important part in the growth and development of California ....and looks forward to many more years of expansion and service."

The fifties ended on a positive note with Cal Water's purchase in September of 1959 of the Mayfair Water Company in Stockton, adding 1,400 new services to Cal Water's largest district, which served 34,021 customers. It was the Company's first significant acquisition since the purchase of Suburban Water Company in 1952.

The event signaled an unpretentious beginning to a dramatic new era for California Water Service Company.

Chapter 24

Releasing the reins...

Ralph Elsman turned 75 years old in July of 1960, his 21st and final year as head of the Company. He relinquished his duties as chairman and chief executive to Robert Minge Brown on Dec. 31, 1960, while continuing his Company association as a director and consultant. At San Jose Water Works, Elsman remained chairman and chief executive until his retirement from that company in 1968.

Elsman's auspicious career as head of Cal Water had resulted in many achievements on behalf of the Company. However, his personal efforts during 1945 in securing the Company stock held by General Water, Gas and Electric Co. undoubtedly was his most dramatic accomplishment. His bold and courageous actions at that time literally saved the Company from its demise at the hands of the eastern financial interests that held control of Cal Water. During his 21-year reign, customer totals nearly tripled from 83,000 in 1940 to 233,197 in 1961. In the same period, annual revenue increased from $2,699,940 to $16,827,895 and net income from $482,825 to $2,131,796. Value of the Company's net plant rose from $16,530,432 to $69,827,895.

His final year, however, would not be without the perennial battles in the districts against the threat of pubic ownership. Seven years after Stockton customers had soundly defeated the City's attempt to acquire the water company, they once again voted to reject a charter amendment for such a purpose in June of 1960. Meanwhile, in the Livermore and Chico Districts, studies were also being made to consider the feasibility of public ownership.

In a letter sent to his future successor, Robert Minge Brown, a few months prior to the Stockton election, Elsman wrote: *"There is no doubt that the Company must strenuously oppose City acquisition in Stockton and in Chico. We have been informed that the City of Stockton has already started its campaign. We cannot afford to lose any more properties in California Water Service Company, and to this end, I am earnestly devoting our attention to opposing any move by any city for the acquisition of our property."*

Elsman noted in his letter that he also was expecting the City of San Jose to make an acquisition attempt on his San Jose Water Works property.

In his final letter to Cal Water shareholders, Elsman proudly announced that the current quarterly dividend being paid *"extended the Company's record of continuous dividend payments on common shares to 29 years."*

Chapter 25

Another extraordinary leader
assumes command...

Robert Minge Brown brought another remarkable period of leadership to Cal Water during his 16 years as chairman and chief executive.

In offering his own assessment of Brown's tenure, former Company Vice President Jeptha Wade, Jr., would comment: *"Bob Brown absolutely would have to be considered one of the major figures among those in the Company's leadership history who made a substantial contribution to our growth and well-being. He had a real concern for people. In addition to his many accomplishments on behalf of the Company, he fought to improve the pension plan and to improve our salaries."*

Brown's life and career were indeed extraordinary. Born in Mobile, Alabama, in 1911, he moved with his family to San Francisco as a young boy, and when he was nine years old, he came to the attention of Stanford psychologist, Lewis Terman, who recruited him for his famous study of 1,500 gifted youngsters with IQ scores higher than 135.

Terman and his Stanford study team would track the lives and careers of his so-called "Termites" for their total life span, measuring their successes and failures both in their private and public lives.

Terman had invited Brown to enroll in Stanford when he was only 13, but Brown commented years later, *"I had better sense than that."* He waited until he was 15 years old before becoming part of the university scene. Brown credited his athletic ability for enabling him to "fit in" at Stanford at such a young age. During one season, he finished second in the mile event during the Pacific Coast Track and Field Championships.

Brown identified with Stanford for much of his life, earning a bachelor's degree in history with great distinction in 1931 at the age of 20. He had been a three-letter athlete at the University and served as student body president while a first-year law student. He was appointed a Rhodes Scholar and studied law at Oxford, graduating in 1934 with a degree in civil law, and would be one of four new associates hired that year by the McCutchen law firm in San Francisco. During World War II, Brown served in naval intelligence on active duty in the Pacific Theater, and following the war, he was discharged with the rank of Lt. Commander. He immediately returned to the McCutchen firm as a partner, specializing in the field of corporate finance and public utility regulation.

During his career, Brown served on the Board of Directors of San Jose Water Works, Hewlett-Packard Co., and the Greyhound Corporation. For many years he was a trustee for both Mills College and Stanford University, and from 1971 to 1976, he served as president of the Stanford Board of Trustees. As part of the arrangement for Brown's services as Cal Water's new chief executive, Elsman permitted him to continue his law practice at McCutchen. Brown retired from McCutchen in 1980, but remained with the firm in a semi-active capacity until March of 1994.

When Brown assumed leadership of Cal Water in 1961, the Company was on the threshold of reaching its strongest financial position since its founding. The Contra Costa sale had been completed earlier in the year, bringing a cash infusion of $12,000,000. Additionally, the purchaser had agreed to assume the Company's long-term refund obligations to Contra Costa developers on new construction

Robert Minge Brown
Chairman of the Board 1961-1981
His tenure as chief executive left a legacy
of leadership which greatly enhanced the
prestige and reputation of California
Water Service Company.

totaling $1,300,000. And finally, the Company was relieved of the costly burden for massive repairs and maintenance that would have been required to bring the District to Cal Water's standard of quality.

Brown later wrote to shareholders, emphasizing that the Company's excellent financial position *"was due in no small measure to a continuation of policies and programs initiated by Mr. Ralph Elsman... during the past two decades."* For Elsman, who had spent a lifetime building a reputation of financial integrity for both himself and his companies, Brown's words must have been especially gratifying.

Following the sale of the Contra Costa District, Brown began personally to negotiate the purchase of four additional systems owned by Pacific Gas & Electric Co. Some 14,000 new customers would be added during March of 1962 through the acquisition of the four water systems in Salinas, Selma, King City and Hamilton City.

The purchase price of $4,650,000 was financed by the proceeds of the Contra Costa sale. In addition to redeeming $1,650,000 in preferred stock, the proceeds also contributed $4,600,000 toward financing Cal Water's construction requirements for the next two years.

A lesson from adversity......

"During our Contra Costa days, Cal Water went through some very, very tough times and we learned some hard lessons. When you live under the type of criticism we had to endure during that period, you have a little less tendency to be critical of others."

Jeptha A. Wade, Jr., retired, 40 years service;
vice president/chief engineer

Chapter 26

Once again the San Jose merger takes center stage...

During the first couple years of his administration, Brown began to put in place the executive team that would serve him during his leadership tenure. Fred Dodge, who was nearing retirement, continued as president, and four new vice presidents were elected — Ralph D. Lindberg, who also served as treasurer; A.V. Lynn, chief engineer; Jeptha A. Wade, Jr., manager of plant development; and C.G. Ferguson, valuation and rate engineer. Laurence L. Camy, a member of the original 1926 Fresno team, was elected an officer and named general manager in charge of operations and construction. Brown's other officers included C.H. Stump, secretary; Ralph Shupe, another Fresno alumnus, controller; and C. A. Larson, Jr., assistant secretary and assistant treasurer.

One of the early actions initiated by Brown as chief executive was to enhance the employee's pension program, working in conjunction with the Company's Utility Workers Union. The plan adopted in 1963 basically supplemented the existing pension benefits by approximately 25 percent of the amount by which the employee's average annual earnings exceeded $4,800 during the five years preceding retirement.

Ever since Christopher T. Chenery's failed attempt in 1928 to acquire the San Jose Water Works for his Cal Water network, discussions on merging the two companies had persisted. In 1963, Brown once again pursued the matter, this time with Ralph Elsman, who had headed the affairs of San Jose Water for more than 28 years. Brown at the time was also a director of San Jose and Elsman's continuing confidant. Brown had been aware that Elsman had long entertained the idea of merging the two companies.

Brown felt the merger presented many advantages for both companies, explaining to Elsman that a combined company would create a very strong water utility with fixed assets of approximately $150,000,000 and a reasonable growth potential. With Cal Water's superior financial strength, Brown suggested that the Company's additional bonding capacity would be available to aid in financing San Jose Water's rapid growth. In addition, he felt a combined organization would make possible the retention and recruiting of experienced operating personnel.

Brown suggested that if Elsman felt the merger was desirable, steps should begin for its implementation. As a target date, Brown suggested the merger proposal be submitted at the regular shareholder meetings of both companies in the spring of 1965. It was felt that before any merger could take place, there had to be some reasonable indication that the City was not likely to acquire San Jose Water's facilities in the immediate future. There was some concern expressed that a merger announcement would precipitate action by the City to begin condemnation of the San Jose Water system. If such action were to occur and municipal ownership negotiations developed, Brown suggested another alternative.

He recommended that a study be made on the feasibility of dividing San Jose Water into two parts with one part sold to the city, incorporating the water facilities within its municipal boundaries. The other portion would cover San Jose Water's facilities in Los Gatos, Cupertino and Saratoga, and be conveyed to California Water Service Company in a transfer of stock. Brown also indicated that before any merger presentations were made to shareholders of both companies, San Jose had to restore its depressed earnings through a rate increase filing with the Public Utilities Commission.

But the plan to join the two companies was once again not to be. Within six months of their merger discussions, Elsman would be devastated by another personal tragedy. His beloved wife, Florence, died at age 58. They had been married 36 years and she had born three of his four children. His daughter Nancy told how deeply distraught her father was after her mother's death: *"My dad really fell apart when my mother died. He just couldn't believe that she would go first. It was very, very difficult for him. They had such a good relationship all those years together."*

In 1967, Elsman retired as head of San Jose Water Works and passed away three years later, just short of his 86th birthday.

Thoughts from a personal friend...

"Bob Brown always took his Cal Water responsibilities very seriously. He ran a tight ship and had incredibly high standards. He respected the people he worked with and always met them more than half way as a gentleman and as a lawyer. Working for him, it was always, 'thank you.' He appreciated the efforts of the people who worked with him and he was a man that was always aware, always considerate of others. Regarding Cal Water, he would say it was his responsibility to see that it was well run and that the shareholders were pleased with their dividends. He was always surrounded by a great group of people at Cal Water. He was a most loving husband and father. He and Gloria were married in 1935 with only $150 in the bank, but a job at McCutchen. They had three sons, and sadly, one died at age 32, only two days after being married. When Gloria died on Jan. l, 1990, they had been married for nearly 55 years. He told me once, 'Eva, I have in Gloria the most perfect, beautiful wife that anyone could ever have.' He took care of her at home when she had cancer and she was in his arms at home when she died."

**Eva Borak, retired, McCutchen law office, 46 years;
personal secretary and friend to Robert Minge Brown**

Officers and managers meeting in San Jose in 1963, the year prior to opening of the new General Office facilities on North First Street. Seated, from left, Fred Dodge, president; Robert Minge Brown, chairman of the Board; Ed Andersen, Stockton manager; Joe Viguier, manager/ construction; Dave Hendrix, Visalia manager; Bud Stump, secretary; Les Carlson, Hermosa-Redondo manager; Ralph Lindberg, vice president/ treasurer; Vern Lynn, vice president/chief engineer. Back row, from left, Jack Rossum, sanitary engineer; Chesley Ferguson, vice president/rates; Bob Lewis, Marysville manager; Laurence Camy, general manager; Amer Stolp, Chico/northern district manager; Bob Tiecke, Livermore manager; Ralph Shupe, controller; Carl Fortner, East Los Angeles manager; Don Winlack, Bakersfield manager; Jeptha Wade, vice president/new business; LaDreu Stolp, Peninsula manager; Harry Kerr, vice president/public relations; Al Larson, assistant secretary.

The East Los Angeles District staff..... early 1960s.

Chapter 27

After 24 years, a new General Office becomes reality...

Early in 1963, Brown directed Jeptha A. Wade, Jr., his vice president and manager of plant development, to begin scouting for a new General Office headquarters site in San Jose. His plan was to construct one of the city's more attractive and functional office facilities to accommodate Cal Water's growing headquarters staff.

For the past 24 years, the Company had occupied an area of 7,500 square feet of rented space on the second floor of the San Jose Water Works building at 374 W. Santa Clara St. During that period, the General Office had met the growing needs of its statewide water systems when customer totals grew from 88,099 to 236,317.

Finding the right location and architect was quite an assignment as Wade would recall: *"My first task was to pinpoint a site that would best serve the Company's needs. We had looked at various locations. At one point we took a map of the Greater San Jose area and plotted where all the employees lived.*

"There was a Cupertino site in which we were very much interested near the location where the Vallco Park Shopping Center was to be developed. Brown, however, did not like the idea of having a Cupertino address. He felt it wouldn't be a good mailing location for dealing with the financial interests back in New York.

"We finally settled on the 9 1/2-acre North First Street site, which we all agreed was a beautiful location. It had easy access to the Bayshore and Highway 17 (now Interstate 880) Freeways, the airport,

and downtown San Jose. So we bought the property, the whole piece for $355,000...about a dollar per square foot.

"After we had interviewed several architects, we settled on Ernest Kump and Associates from Palo Alto. He was the architect for the Foothill College complex in Los Altos and had a good reputation. We reviewed our ideas with his staff, explaining that we wanted a design and layout that would speak to California, something also that would speak to our business of water.

"We wanted to project and improve our image since we had been hidden so long behind the face of San Jose Water Works within their headquarters facilities. Nobody knew of California Water Service Company.

"We also decided to work with a landscape architect from the very start of planning rather than having the landscaper dress up something that had already been built. We wanted the actual landscape design to be part of the original architectural layout, so we hired Robert Royston, a successor to Thomas Church, a famous landscape architect in San Francisco.

"Before the plans were even created, Brown, Dodge, Kump and I worked with the landscape architect in reviewing preliminary sketches to finally arrive at a good concept for the outside area. On Dec. 27, 1963, Cal Water issued a news release officially announcing that the Company would begin construction of new headquarters facilities on North First Street in San Jose using five acres of a 9 1/2-acre site.

"The plans called for the design and construction of three single-story structures totaling 21,000 sq. ft. with exposed aggregate, vertical redwood siding, and glass exteriors. Shake roofs were to be used to give added texture to the general layout, which included a central patio with reflecting pool and fountains."

By November of 1964, the North First Street headquarters

complex was ready for occupancy, and personnel from engineering, human resources, accounting, water quality, stores, purchasing, rates and the executive staff would complete the move to their new offices by the end of the year. A major feature of the complex was the Company's modern new laboratory, which would be recognized as one of the finest water quality testing facilities in the state.

To honor and recognize Ralph Elsman's past service to the Company, Brown had reserved the northwest corner office in the new executive building for the former chairman's exclusive use. Elsman, who was nearing 80 and was still mourning the loss of his wife earlier in the year, attended the open house and occupied his new office for the first and only time. For the next year, the corner office, with the name Ralph Elsman on the door, would remain dark.

In 1964, California Water Service built its present General Office facilities on a 9 1/2-acre site at 1720 North First St. in San Jose, California. The complex was designed by Ernest Kump and Associates of Palo Alto with a California-style architecture, and remains today as esthetically beautiful and contemporary as when first constructed. Shown here is the attractive garden pool area along with one of two landscaped atrium areas which adorn the facilities. During subsequent years, several additions to the complex have been built, including construction of the 15,800-sq.-ft. engineering-water quality building in 1992.

Cal Water's new General Office complex on North First Street in San Jose was nearing completion during the final months of 1964 as directors held their first meeting in the new Board Room facilities. Shown here in this Nov. 18, 1964, photograph are, from left, Directors Albert W. Beall, Fred L. Dodge, Fred J. Oehler, A. Crawford Greene, Sr., Robert Minge Brown, Ralph Elsman, C.B. Leib, Paul E. Holden and Frank F. Walker.

Engineering and water quality departments assemble for mid-1960s photo in the new N. First Street facilities. Standing in foreground is Chief Engineer Vern Lynn. 1. Bill Vickers, 2. Carey Neal, Jr., 3. Bill Kirmayer, 4. Otto Neilsen, 5. Angelo Belleci, 6. Les Saxe, 7. Dick Menden, 8. Andy Soule, 9. Ralph Steiber, 10. Ben Villarruz, 11. John Anderson, 12. Vern Lynn, 13. Dan McLean, 14. Bob Navarrete, 15. Dave Heninger, 16. Jack Prendergast, 17. George Coolidge, 18. Joy Tripoli, 19. Ann Taylor, 20. Primo Villarruz, 21. Jack Rossum, 22. Mike Calleri, 23. Jim Nervig, 24. Ernie Centofante, 25. Morris Quanrud, 26. Dorothy Shepard, 27. Bob Smith, 28. Parker Robinson

Chapter 28

Strength through leadership, financial stability...

The early years of Brown's leadership still would encounter the ongoing efforts by city officials seeking municipal ownership of the Company's water systems. Toward this end, discussions and feasibility studies in various stages had been under way in Selma, Livermore, Chico, San Mateo and Oroville.

The City of Selma advanced to the stage of a city-wide election in November of 1965 when voters rejected the City's plans to purchase the water system. In the other districts, Cal Water continued to remain resolute in countering all existing takeover attempts.

By 1973, Stockton District was the only Company system that remained under serious threat of condemnation. But in a city-wide election held in November of that year, Stockton citizens once again voted overwhelmingly to reject municipal ownership of the Company's local water district.

In recognition of Cal Water's growing financial strength, Standard and Poor's was preparing to raise the Company's bond rating to AA+, which would be the highest given to any California utility. Buoyed by the Company's increased stature in the financial community, Brown continued his search for excellent water properties in which to invest or acquire. In 1964, he sought to obtain a block of stock in the Dominguez Water Corporation, a private utility operating in proximity to the Company's Hermosa-Redondo District, pursuing the effort through Frank Walker, a partner in Dean Witter & Co. and a member of the Cal Water Board since 1958. Following an investigation, Walker would report back to Brown that the only substantial block of Dominguez shares was controlled by members of the Dominguez Estate Company and these shares, he said, were not for sale. Brown's inquiry had been prompted by a Dominguez public offering of some 70,000 shares during the previous year. Walker explained that the Dominguez group had "very reluctantly" sold the 70,000 shares for the sole purpose of creating an outside market.

The following year, Cal Water was successful in acquiring another water system with purchase of the Crest Water Company in Bakersfield. The new system added 1,650 customers to the District's year-end totals of 34,000. The number of services statewide had reached 238,841.

At the end of 1965, Fred Dodge retired as president, culminating a 39-year career. For 25 years, Dodge served as a strong and forceful lieutenant, first to Elsman and then later to Brown. He would remain a member of the Board for the next ten years. Dodge was a product of his time and his style of leadership without question invoked trepidation among many of the employees. He was feared by many, but respected by all. Parker Robinson, who had worked closely with Dodge as an assistant chief engineer, would comment years later:

"Fred Dodge was a strict and tough-minded man with a reputation for being a very fair boss. He didn't ask you to do things he didn't think you could do, but he expected you to do what you were supposed to do. And, he would recognize you when you did something right. I had great respect for him.

"He had a sense of humor, too. I remember going in for an employee review and the only comment he had was, 'You don't smile enough.'"
Before he retired, Elsman had paid Dodge the highest of compliments when he confided to a district manager, *"If it hadn't been for Fred Dodge, the Company would never have grown to where it was."*

Dodge was succeeded by Ralph D. Lindberg as president with Brown continuing as chief executive and chairman. Since joining the Company in 1957, Lindberg had held a number of executive positions, including that of assistant treasurer, treasurer and vice president. A former IRS agent and Certified Public Accountant, he had attended the University of Utah and its law school and held degrees in both accounting and law. In 1958, he had replaced Harlan Hulick after Hulick died suddenly of heart failure at age 50. Hulick was one of the successful Fresno alumni to join the Company in 1926. One of his fellow employees from the original Fresno team, Laurence Camy, the Company's general manager, would also die unexpectedly several years later at age 61. He suffered a heart attack following a presentation on civil defense before water district engineers in San Francisco.

By the mid-1960s, Brown had already begun to build a Board membership that would reflect his goal to broaden the prestige and reputation of California Water Service Company. Elsman's directors had primarily consisted of businessmen and attorneys who were well-known and respected in the local community, whereas, Brown would now select Board candidates not only from a wider Bay Area pool of professional talent, but also from distinguished representatives who resided in districts served by the Company.

Brown's first board selection in 1962 was Paul E. Holden of Menlo Park, professor emeritus of industrial management at Stanford University. This would be followed in 1967 by the election of L. W. Lane, Jr., publisher of *Sunset* magazine, president of Lane Publishing & Book of Menlo Park and a resident of Portola Valley, a Cal Water service area. As the decade came to a close, Brown announced that Karl Wente, president of Wente Bros. winery in Livermore, had been nominated for Board membership. Livermore had been a Cal Water service area since the 1920s.

Chapter 29

Advancing forward through initiative and innovation...

T hroughout its history as a publicly held company, Cal Water has aggressively taken an active role in meeting its public responsibilities and corporate challenges. The steadfast efforts of Cal Water's engineers to ensure a safe, potable water supply continues to this day.

Although groundwater has always served as a major source for the Company, it was apparent from the very beginning that alternate supplies would always be needed, always be sought. In 1928, the Chenery or Mallard Project with its reservoir, pumping plant and treatment facilities was the first major undertaking by Company engineers to develop a major source of surface water. The project would meet the needs of Contra Costa District customers for nearly 30 years.

When salt water intrusion and declining groundwater levels threatened the Company's well supply in the Los Angeles Basin, the engineers again met the challenge. Their aggressive action to preserve groundwater rights eventually resulted in Cal Water securing a supplemental surface water supply from the governmental water agency serving the metropolitan area.

In more recent years, Company engineers have been active participants in the Bay Area Water Users Association in contract negotiations with the San Francisco Water Department, the water supplier for the Company's Peninsula Districts. The contracts not only protect the Company's water rights to San Francisco's reservoir

1970

supply, but also place limits on wholesale water rates charged to the Company for construction of San Francisco's future facilities.

By 1961, the State of California had begun construction of its $1.6 billion State Water Project, designed to capture and transport water from the State's northern area to the more arid regions of central and southern California. The project included construction of the Oroville Dam, the San Luis Reservoir, and statewide transmission and aqueduct facilities. Once completed, the project delivered a major supply of surface water to Cal Water districts in Los Altos, Livermore, Oroville, Bakersfield and the Los Angeles area. Again, Cal Water engineers were on the scene, working closely with local water agencies in each district to negotiate contracts to meet the water needs of Company customers. As a result of the State Water Project, district underground water levels improved significantly as demand on well production lessened.

In the Stockton District, Cal Water engineers worked closely with the Stockton-East Water District to guarantee the purchase of surface water supplies from the area's New Hogan Reservoir. Salt water intrusion from the California Delta had endangered the underground supply before the arrival of the surface water from Stockton-East.

The dedication and professionalism of the Company's nine chief engineers and their staffs had contributed immeasurably to the success of Cal Water during the past 78 years. Jeptha A. Wade, Jr., had the longest tenure as chief engineer, serving 21 years. Earlier, his father, Jeptha A.Wade, Sr., had served in the position for 11 years.

In the fall of 1967, Cal Water made a momentous entry into the electronic age with the conversion of its billing operations to a data processing system affecting nearly a quarter-million customers.

S.M. DiMartino, who at the time was in charge of the

Chief Engineers
California Water Service Company

E. K. "Kirby" Barnum	1926 - 1932
H. A. "Bucky" Harris	(acting) 1932
Jeptha A. Wade, Sr.	1933 - 1944
H. A. "Bucky" Harris	1944 - 1952
Vern Lynn	1952 - 1966
Jeptha A. Wade, Jr.	1966 - 1987
David C. Heninger	1987 - 1990
Robert R. Guzzetta	1990 - 1996
Michael J. Rossi	1997 -

Company's Central Billing Office in Stockton, was chosen to head up the program as Manager of Data Processing. Ray Worrell, an experienced computer programmer from Crocker Bank, was hired as his assistant.

DiMartino had been with the Company since 1954 after graduating from the University of Southern California. When he first applied for a job in the Company's East Los Angeles District, he remembers telling the office manager that he also spoke Spanish, having studied the language in high school. He thought this might be an asset in getting the job. DiMartino remembers how he became quickly aware of the mind set of the times when the office manager informed him, *"We only speak English here."*

The mechanical Addressograph operations of the Central Billing Office in Stockton were gradually phased out during 1968 under the direction of John Simpson. Simultaneously, DiMartino's new data processing operation was undertaking the conversion process in rented office space in Santa Clara, within a couple miles of the General Office on North First Street in San Jose. Together with DiMartino and Worrell, the original data processing team included Gloria Villareal, Bob Ray, Bruce Keniston and Rose Barrales, who all remained with the Company for 32 years.

The entire conversion of 360,000 customers to electronic billing incorporating the use of IBM cards was completed by December 1968, on time and on budget. By 1972, the data processing operation had moved from its rented offices to newly constructed space at the North First Street headquarters complex.

Chapter 30

"I took a one-semester course
and got bit!"

As the Company's billing program moved rapidly into the electronic age during the early 1970s, engineering also was taking its own initial steps into the world of computers. A major player in this effort was Parker Robinson, a Stanford engineering graduate who had been a California Water Service Company mainstay in the engineering department since joining the Company following World War II. He was chiefly responsible for developing the Company's program to computerize engineering and district operations. Robinson vividly recalls traveling the early path to becoming "computer savvy:"

"I remember seeing the Hewlett-Packard hand-held calculator when it first came out and I thought to myself, how absolutely marvelous. It cost around $400 then, but you can buy one today for about $10.

"Chesley Ferguson, the vice president in charge of rates at the time, had decided to buy one for the Company to assist him in his rate cases. It was known as a programmable calculator. You could write programs and do a number of calculations and 'Fergie' knew that I was interested in things like that. When he received his calculator, he called me over to his office to explain how programs could be written and I thought it was tremendous. I had absolutely no idea what a computer program was... no concept at all. But I wanted to learn.

"I signed up at Foothill College for a course in computer programming. This was during the early 1970s when schools did not have computer departments. Courses of this sort were handled as part

of the electrical engineering curriculum. So I took a one-semester course in programming...and I got bit!

"It was very interesting, and not too long afterwards, Jep Wade, our chief engineer, and Ralph Lindberg, the president, decided that engineering should have some type of computer capability."

1976
Local and District Managers

Bakersfield .... Don Winlack (Dist. Mgr.)

Bear Gulch .... Al Stregger (Dist. Mgr.)

Chico/Hamilton City .... Gene Grant (Dist. Mgr.)

Dixon .... John Droll (Local Mgr.)

East Los Angeles .... Eldon Shadrick (Dist. Mgr.)

Hermosa-Redondo .... Jim Cantrell (Dist. Mgr.)

King City .... Del Lombard (Local Mgr.)

Livermore .... Bob Tiecke (Dist. Mgr.)

Los Altos-Suburban .... Gary Garibaldi (Local Mgr.)

Marysville .... Mike Camy (Local Mgr.)

Oroville .... Chuck Staley (Local Mgr.)

Palos Verdes .... Chuck Nollenberger (Dist. Mgr.)

Salinas .... Dean Wagoner (Dist. Mgr.)

San Mateo/San Carlos .... Barney Tumey (Dist. Mgr.)

Selma .... Bill Webster (Local Mgr.)

So. San Fran./Broadmoor ... Doug Southworth (Local Mgr.)

Stockton .... Bob Lewis (Dist. Mgr.)

Visalia .... Ken Dow (Dist. Mgr.)

Willows .... Rob Thompson (Local Mgr.)

Robinson explained everyone was aware that computer work was under way over in the billing department. But the new data processing area was operating at that time from a completely separate facility, away from the General Office site. There was little contact between billing and the other Company departments including engineering.

"We didn't even know the people in billing, much less have access to their computer equipment," Robinson said. *"Lindberg gave us the go ahead to sign up for a timeshare computer system working with a company in Mountain View that had an HP mini-computer. Thus, we were able to access that computer over the telephone line using modems and an old-style teletype machine. We installed our teletype in a small back room in the water quality laboratory and that was engineering's first computer operation. It was an inauspicious beginning."*

Robinson said Jack Rossum, the water quality director, also had a real interest in computers and how they might help him in his lab work. Thus, his offer of lab space to accommodate engineering's teletype equipment.

"In those days you couldn't buy word processors and spread sheets," Robinson said. *"They hadn't been invented. So in order to do any computer work we had to write our own programs. With my one semester of schooling behind me, I wrote some programs for the engineering department that we ended up using for years. Rossum and I collaborated on writing one of the first programs because his calculus was better than mine. It was a program involving hydraulic analysis to compute flows and pressures. We used this for many years until much fancier stuff came along.*

"I also wrote a program for calculating and printing out cost estimates for subdivision development. It gave the developer a cost estimate on installing the water system, thus making it easier for the engineering staff. Lindberg had encouraged me and was supportive of

my computer activities. We had a lot of talks and he asked me many questions because he wanted to be sure that something was going to come of all this—that it just wasn't something pouring money down a rat hole. I personally didn't know of all the potential for the computer, but I guess I convinced him that we could do something useful."

By the late seventies, Cal Water was beginning to see the computer's potential for engineering. The Company bought a system that would monitor a water district's entire operations over telephone lines, reporting back production data, emergencies and other vital information.

"The first computer control system was installed in the Bear Gulch field office," Robinson said. *"We bought a Data General minicomputer — a big blue box that sat upright on the floor, and things began to progress from there. At first I think the district people were a bit afraid of the computer when we began to install the monitoring systems. I would take the computer out to the district and give an instruction course to staff members, telling them how to use it. Some were frightened by it, but others really took to it.*

"At the General Office it was same thing. Some of the engineers took to it like fish to water, but a few really had problems with it. They would be scared of it. Some would make every effort to avoid using the computer, asking the engineering secretary to run the computer to do estimates and other functions. After time, though, most of the engineering staff and people in the districts took to the computer once they realized how much easier it would make their jobs.

"After we had installed the Bear Gulch system, the Company agreed that engineering should go off computer timesharing at the General Office and okayed the purchase of our first permanent computer at the General Office. We felt that engineering's computer should be an open system to get everyone at GO acquainted with its

use. We invited anybody at anytime in the General Office to come in and use the computer along with all the engineers who were doing their hydraulic programs and such. I wrote a program entitled Biorhythm Analysis based upon people's birthdays. It was a popular thing at that time. So the ladies in accounting and the other secretaries from throughout GO would come into the engineering computer room during the lunch hour and run biorhythm charts for themselves. That's how they became familiar with the computer. If they ran into problems, they would come to us and we would help them. The engineering computer was always open for anyone's use.

"After we had established our first mini-computer in the office, it was decided that someone other than myself should have personal knowledge of how things worked. So Rob Guzzetta and Mike Rossi were selected to attend Data General school to learn the ins and outs of the computer. They both became pretty knowledgeable. The rest is history, as they say."

A special tribute...

"Parker Robinson was very instrumental both in the computerization of the water systems and the computerization of the engineering department, including the supervisory control systems. 'Robby' was probably in his fifties at the time, learning all this and going to computer school, and I believe he even built his own home computer. Then he worked to convince the Company that we should put a computer system in Bear Gulch. It was the foundation he laid that was extremely valuable in getting us to where we are now."

Robert R. Guzzetta, vice president,
Engineering and Water Quality 2004

Chapter 31

Building the Company's future...

The purchase of the Palos Verdes Water Company in 1970 was the largest acquisition by California Water Service Company since its formation in 1926. It added 17,500 new services and became the Company's 22nd operating system, bringing the number of total statewide customers to 268,828. The District was acquired for $3 million cash from the Great Lakes Carbon Company and financed through the sale of first mortgage bonds. Located on the Palo Verdes Peninsula in Los Angeles County, it served one of the more affluent residential areas in southern California and included three incorporated cities — Palos Verdes Estates, Rolling Hills Estates and Rolling Hills, in addition to a large unincorporated county area. Today, a fourth peninsula city, Rancho Palos Verdes, is also part of the Company's service area. During Brown's first nine years as chief executive, approximately 33,000 new customers had been added through acquisitions. Brown would announce that the Palos Verdes acquisition was "an important development in building for the Company's future." Within a month after the new purchase, an important chapter of the Company's story came to an end with the death of Ralph Elsman on July 2,1970, three weeks prior to his 86th birthday.

Two eminent San Francisco Peninsula residents, Dr. William E. Ayer and Dr. Robert J. Glaser, M.D. were named to the Cal Water Board in 1972. They replaced Fred Oehler, vice president of Wells Fargo Bank, and Frank Walker, general partner of Dean Witter and

Co. Combined, the two retiring directors had contributed 45 years of distinguished service to the Company. Dr. Ayer of Los Altos Hills brought to the Board extensive business experience and a prestigious background. A management consultant and private investor, he was founder and president of Applied Technology Inc. before the firm became a division of Itek Corp. He had gained an international reputation in the electronics field.

Dr. Glaser was president and director of the Henry J. Kaiser Family Foundation and had a distinguished career as dean of the School of Medicine and vice president for medical affairs of Stanford University. His election as a director initiated a new Company policy by which a medical doctor would always be represented on the Board to advise on matters relating to water quality.

By 1974, another Board vacancy had occurred through the retirement of Paul E. Holden, an esteemed director for 12 years. He was replaced by Dr. Robert K. Jaedicke, professor of accounting and associate and later dean of the Stanford Graduate School of Business. Dean Jaedicke had authored several books and numerous professional articles on accounting and was a valued addition to the Board.

During the early 1970s, a major breakthrough had taken place regarding Company efforts to establish a more unified and realistic tax assessment of its utility property. For years, Company property taxes had been determined on the basis of individual assessments by county assessors in each of Cal Water's 22 operating districts. The varying assessments resulted in the Company's total property being taxed on a higher basis than the State's gas and electric utilities, which were under jurisdiction of the State Board of Equalization.

C. A. Larson, Jr., who at the time was the Company's assistant treasurer and assistant secretary, worked closely with state assessors and the Board of Equalization to establish guidelines for a uniform method of appraisal. As a result, Company property tax assessments were reduced by approximately $400,000 over a three-year period following the adoption of the new guidelines.

From gold coins, to cash, to checks...

"In the Company's very early days, the bylaws had provided that members of the Board of Directors be paid for their services in gold coin. A member of the accounting department was given the responsibility of going to the bank and paying the directors in gold coin following each meeting. After gold had been phased out as legal tender, the Company always paid the director's fee in cash following each meeting. One of our people in the accounting department would go to the bank and get $50 bills to pay the directors. On one occasion someone picked the employee's pocket on his return from the bank and we had to make a hurried trip back to the bank before the meeting ended. We eventually went to issuing their fee in checks."

Al Larson, retired, corporate secretary;
Company service, 1950-1983

Chapter 32

A new style of management...

As Cal Water was approaching its 50th anniversary, major leadership changes were well under way that would impact the Company's future for the next 25 years. And a new style of management was emerging.

In 1975, former president Fred L. Dodge resigned as a member of the Board of Directors upon reaching the mandatory retirement age of 75. In recognition of his major contributions to the Company during his 50 years of service, he was designated director emeritus. J.J. Viguier, vice president for operations and construction, also retired that year after a 43-year career. He had been a utility worker for the Pacific Water Company, which was acquired by Cal Water in 1932.

C.H. "Bud" Stump, who had joined the Company as a field worker in 1950, was elected executive vice president and a member of the Board in June 1975. He had previously served as secretary-treasurer of the Company. Stump's first 25 years had prepared him well for his new role in charge of Company operations. But it was his relaxed personal demeanor embodied in his management style that would make a lasting impact on friends and co-workers.

A native of Los Gatos, California, Stump was born in 1925, one year before the founding of his future company. He attended Los Gatos High School and received a bachelor's degree in history from the University of California at Berkeley in 1945.

After service with the Merchant Marines, Stump received a

number of job offers, but had made the decision to apply with Cal Water at the suggestion of a friend. Stump explained, *"I wanted to work for a company that would give me the feeling I was contributing in some way to my fellow man through personal service. I felt that Cal Water might be a good choice for me. Jack Call, the Company's personnel director, told me there were no openings at the time in the General Office that called for a university graduate. But he did suggest I consider starting in the San Mateo District as a field worker and see where it would lead. I said I'd love to take the job to get acquainted with the Company. I have always been grateful for my experience in the districts, since I discovered later in my career that it had allowed me to empathize more readily with the needs and challenges being faced by our employees."*

In addition to his work as an operations maintenance worker, Stump's career in the districts also included service as foreman in Bear Gulch, clerk trainee in San Mateo, and finally chief clerk in Stockton.

"When I came into the General Office later in the fifties, I remember one of the officers telling me that he didn't think Cal Water was a good company for a young person like myself 'because it didn't have much future.' Of course I stayed, and I'm certainly glad he was proven wrong."

Many former employees have commented upon the strict, inflexible atmosphere that had prevailed within management during the early years. All agreed it reflected the times in general, when business leaders seemed less empathetic, more stringent than present day.

"Earlier times did indeed reflect a more rigid management style," Stump explained. *"However, it never detracted from the Company's ongoing pursuit of professionalism and excellence, and for the desire always to do the right thing in service to the customer. The officers, supervisors and employees of those early days always were*

dedicated to doing the very best in performing their jobs."

John Simpson, retired, assistant secretary and manager of new business with 40 years service in the General Office and in the districts, comments: *"I cannot emphasize enough how important Bud Stump's role was in balancing the management style of those early days with a genuine interest in the employee. His efforts created a family atmosphere among us all."*

Words of counsel after 50 years...

"Whenever I have talked to young employees and they ask me about my career and my successes, I always tell them I had only one formula for getting ahead:

- ***Always** try to do the very best job that can be done <u>in each role you are playing</u>;*
- ***Always** keep the interest of the Company at heart;*
- ***Always** keep the interest of our customers at heart; and*
- ***Always** maintain the highest level of service to ensure the reputation of our Company.*

If you want to advance in the Company, always do the best job possible and do not be intimidated by others who may feel you are trying too hard. I say never get in the position of being brought down to someone else's level. Just do the best job that you can do and don't worry about what your next position will be. If you worry about that, you won't do justice to your current position."

C. H. "Bud" Stump, retired, chairman and CEO;
50 years service starting Aug. 1, 1950;
operations maintenance worker, San Mateo District

Ralph D. Lindberg
Chief Executive Officer 1977-1985
Chairman 1981-1990
*His distinguished 33-year
career with the Company was
highlighted by his innovations
in financial management,
employee benefits and
regulatory matters. He was
recognized nationally through
his election as president of
the National Association
of Water Companies.*

C. H. ("Bud") Stump
Chief Executive Officer 1986-1992
Chairman 1991-1995
*From operations
maintenance worker
to chairman and chief
executive officer during
a Cal Water career
spanning 50 years.*

Harry T. Kerr
_Retired in 1976 after many years of
dedicated service on behalf of the
Company, first as a public relations
consultant and later as vice president for
public affairs. His keen ability to interpret
and resolve community matters
contributed significantly to the Company's
high standing throughout the districts._

Harold C. Ulrich
_The Company's long-held reputation
for fiscal responsibility was carried
forth through his acumen and
professionalism while serving as
controller and later as vice president,
chief financial officer and treasurer.
He retired in 1994 after 32 years of
distinguished service._

Executive Building staff, June 1976 — _Front row, from left, Al Larson,
Harry Kerr, Ralph D. Lindberg, Robert Minge Brown, C. H. "Bud" Stump.
Second row, from left, Marguerite St. Aubin, Roberta Nelson, Ida White,
Velma Potter, Phyllis Lovoi, Betty Yazel, Marion Frasier, Dianne Brown.
Third row, from left, Ken Roed, Jeptha Wade, Ken Kilby, Rudy Calica,Tom
Lorenzen, George Wilkus, Ed Catey, Hal Emmerich._

Staff members from accounting, purchasing and stores are shown in this 1976 gathering at the North First Street General Office. Front row, from left, Ray Zern, Harold Ulrich, Debbie Campbell, Bill Lewis, Donna Farrell, Annette White, Van Rojas; second row, from left, Jayne Lally, Nalda Sorisso, Gila Torres, Dorothy Shepard, Joan Newman,Wayne Newbern; Back row, from left, Dick Trueblood, Bev Hayes, Joanne Whitlock, Ray Bramlette, Harold Saunders.

Most of the Company's engineering staff were present for this 1976 photograph taken at General Office, 1720 North First Street, San Jose. In front row, from left, Pat Requa, Sherry Tollas, Parker Robinson, Dave Heninger, Jeptha Wade, Jr., Jack Prendergast, Andy Soule, Christine McFarlane; second row, from left, Fred Rios, Roy Lopaus, Carey Neal, Jr., Ernie Centofante, Les Saxe, Bob Smith, Bob Navarrete, Roy Nelson; back row, from left, Bob Momand, Fernando Teran, George Damarell, Mike Sheehy, James Simunovich, Dave McIntyre, Morris Quanrud, Frank Weldon, Bill Vickers, Jose Mendes.

Data processing staff 1976, front row, from left, Elvira Mazzei, Judy Seifert, Bonnie Toole, Michele Lucchesi, Gloria Villareal, Margo McElroy. Back row, from left, Nelda Lofton, S.M. DiMartino, Ray Worrell, Jim Welton, Rose Barrales.

The mid-1970s was a transitional period for Cal Water's top leadership. Fred L. Dodge was retiring as a director; Robert Minge Brown was stepping down as chief executive officer, a post being filled by then-President Ralph D. Lindberg; C. H. Stump had been appointed executive vice president; and Harry Kerr was retiring as vice president of public affairs. This 1976 photograph depicts the group appearing at a General Office gathering of officers, managers and retirees. Front row, from left, Dodge, Kerr, Lindberg, Brown, Stump and Al Stregger. Second row, from left, Al Larson, Jeptha Wade, Jr., Dave Heninger, Gene Grant, Ken Kilby, Bill Lewis, Hal Ulrich and LaDreu Stolp. Third row, from left, Ray Worrell, Van Rojas, Ken Dow, Andy Soule, Les Saxe, Frank Weldon, George Wilkus, Ed Catey, S.M. DiMartino, Sam Volonte and Chuck Nollenberger. Fourth row, from left, C. G. Ferguson, Jim Cantrell, Ray Zern, Barney Tumey, Dave Hendrix, Dean Wagoner, Bob Tiecke, Parker Robinson, Hal Emmerich and Ralph Shupe. Fifth row, from left, Ken Roed, Les Carlson, unidentified, Jack Prendergast, Eldon Shadrick, Rudy Calica, Dick Menden, Dick Trueblood, Don Winlack and Bob Lewis.

Chapter 33

Fifty years and growing...

T he Company celebrated a half-century of service during 1976, commemorated by a state legislative resolution recognizing the Company's water service contribution to more than one million California residents.

It was Robert Minge Brown's 16th and final year as chief executive, and by any measure, his leadership tenure was recognized as a major success. During his reign, customer totals statewide increased by 58,600, and annual revenue rose from $16,827,895 to $46,309,000. Revenue in 1976 had increased a record 20 percent over the preceding year and net income rose to $5,835,000, or a record 16 percent. The Company's new General Office complex, built in 1964, was undoubtedly among Brown's proudest achievements during his time as chief executive.

Approximately $12.4 million in plant replacements and improvements during 1976 had included the construction of Company filter plants in the Oroville and Bear Gulch Districts. In addition, $1 million had been spent to purchase the Garden Water system in Bakersfield with 2,600 accounts, nearly half of the 6,300 customers added during the year. Cal Water was indeed entering its next half-century in forward motion, bolstered by a strong financial foundation. Upon Brown's retirement, Ralph D. Lindberg, president of the Company since 1966, became chief executive officer with Brown remaining on the Board as chairman.

With Stump serving as his right hand in charge of Company operations, Lindberg began forming his own executive team which included Harold C. Ulrich, elected vice president and treasurer; C. A. Larson, Jr., secretary; Harold J. Emmerich, assistant secretary and assistant treasurer and Gerald F. Feeney, controller. Harry T. Kerr, vice president of public affairs, retired after 24 years of service, first as a consultant and later as a Company officer and was replaced by Kenneth J. Roed, who held the title of assistant to the president.

The Company was saddened by the sudden death of Board member Karl L. Wente in January of 1977. He was a highly respected director since 1970 and was active in community affairs, including service as a trustee for the California State Colleges and Universities. His vacancy on the Board would not be filled until the following June when Robert W. Foy, an esteemed civic and business leader in the City of Stockton, was selected as a Company director. Nineteen years later, Foy helped usher in a dynamic new era for California Water Service Company as chairman of the Board.

During 1977, for the first time in Company history, water rationing would be imposed upon Cal Water's customers as a result of a severe two-year drought. From 1976 through November of 1977, California had experienced the lowest two-year rainfall recorded in modern times.

A 25-percent mandatory reduction in water use was required on the San Francisco Peninsula for customers in the Company's San Mateo, South San Francisco, San Carlos and Bear Gulch Districts. In the Company's southern California districts of Palos Verdes, East Los Angeles and Hermoso-Redondo, a 10-percent reduction was required. In other areas of the state, stringent water conservation rules were imposed upon all customers to meet the state emergency.

The drought finally broke during the 1977-1978 winter season following severe storms that restored the state's reservoir supplies to normal levels. As a result of the drought, which had been the most serious in recent years, the Company would undertake an aggressive, ongoing program in support of customer conservation.

A new member of Ralph Lindberg's executive team joined the Company early in 1977 when Donald L. Houck was elected vice president in charge of regulatory matters. Before joining the Company, Houck had been a member of the supervisory staff of the California Public Utilities Commission for 17 years. He replaced Ed F. Catey, who had served the Company since 1973 in the regulatory rate-making role.

The year would also mark the Company's first venture into a management opportunity involving the operation of a city-owned water system. A contract was signed with the City of Bakersfield authorizing the Company to assume management of the new City-owned water system serving 4,100 customers. The City had purchased the water operations of Tenneco West, a major land developer in the Bakersfield area.

By 1980, the Company had grown to 310,000 customers served through 20 operating districts. Company growth during the opening years of the 1980s, however, would be hampered to a large extent by high interest rates as the prime rate soared to 21 percent in December of 1980, slowing the development of new subdivisions. However, for the total decade, Cal Water would gain 43,500 customers, including 9,700 new services added through the acquisition of four water systems. The largest of these was the Westlake Water Company purchase in 1983, which increased customer totals by 4,400 new services. The water system was located in southern California in an upscale, planned community developed on a 12,000-acre ranch in Thousand Oaks in Ventura County. The prior year, the Company had made two acquisitions — the North Los Altos Water Company with 1,350 services and the Salinas Hills water system with 750 services. The fourth acquisition came with purchase of the Water West Corporation, a water system with 3,200 customers in Monterey County near Salinas.

For the first time in 12 years, the Company would once again face a municipal election in November 1985 as the City of Oroville sought voter approval to purchase the water system. Following a campaign that brought widespread community support for the Company, Oroville citizens decisively rejected the city's ownership proposal by a 2-1 vote.

Chapter 34

High technology rules the day...

T hroughout the eighties, dramatic advancements in technology were embraced by Cal Water to enhance programs in water quality, engineering and information systems.

Public concern for the safety of the nation's drinking water supply had risen, resulting in new state and federal regulations for monitoring the drinking water supply. Extensive testing of all community water systems was required to determine if volatile organic chemicals (VOCs), commonly referred to as man-made chemicals, had contaminated the groundwater supply.

Of the Company's 500 wells in operation, testing during the period had determined that only a few well stations had been contaminated above allowable levels. These wells were taken out of service until treatment could be installed. Innovative treatment programs under the direction of Raymond Taylor, the Company's head of water quality at the time, were initiated to remove contaminants from the underground aquifers. In the Selma District, a successful treatment operation was put in place in 1987 using a carbon adsorption process to remove the man-made chemical DBCP from the groundwater. This was the first use of this treatment anywhere in California.

Meanwhile, in the Chico District, another unique treatment procedure developed by the Company, known as an "air stripper," which incorporated a water-aeration process, was placed in operation. It extracted the VOC contaminant known as PCE, which had been detected in an area of the City's groundwater supply. By 1990, the Company would have in operation up to 12 well treatment facilities in Chico, Selma, Bakersfield and Salinas. They employed either granular-activated carbon (GAC) or air-stripping procedures to remove VOC contaminants from groundwater.

Information systems had also incorporated new technology to improve operations of the Company's billing program. Customer bills were modified to provide more detailed information on water consumption and costs. Each bill would now include the customer's 12-month water consumption history to permit closer monitoring of water usage, a feature especially important during dry years. Monthly billing operations became completely automated, printing 360,000 continuous form bills on a high-speed printer that cut, folded and prepared each bill for mailing in zip code order.

In 1986, meter reading had also gone high tech. Company service personnel were equipped with hand-held computers that recorded the monthly water use of 260,000 metered customers. The readings, stored in the portable computers, were transmitted daily from each district to the Company's data processing center and its mainframe computer located at the General Office.

By 1983, the engineering department was also moving aggressively to make use of the rapid advances in technology for improving district operations. The Company maintained its ongoing program to place computer technology in the larger districts to achieve system monitoring through remote control capability.

Chapter 35

A decade of change...

T he 1980s brought a number of executive changes through retirements and appointments at the Company's highest levels. In October 1981, Robert Minge Brown stepped down as chairman of the board and was replaced by Ralph Lindberg, who had been president since 1966. Brown continued as a Company director and Lindberg as chief executive. C.H. "Bud" Stump was elected president and chief operating officer.

At the Company's annual meeting in April 1982, the by-laws were amended, providing for an additional director. Elected to fill the position was Roscoe Moss, Jr., chairman of the Roscoe Moss Company, a California firm long active in the water development field. Moss had recently become a substantial shareholder in the Company, acquiring approximately 10 percent of the Company's outstanding common stock. His holdings, which had been acquired from Warren Buffett, Omaha's legendary investor, represented the largest block held by a Company shareholder at that time.

In July of 1983, C.A. Larson, Jr., secretary, and Harold C. Emmerich, assistant secretary and assistant treasurer, retired after serving the Company for 33 and 34 years, respectively. Lester E. Saxe was elected to succeed Larson as secretary.

The following year, George W. Adrian, vice president and director of water quality, also retired and was replaced by Raymond H. Taylor.

Adrian, a past chairman of the California-Nevada Section of the American Water Works Association, was a nationally prominent water quality engineer who had received numerous awards in his profession. Taylor had worked 17 years in water research and treatment for the U.S. Environmental Protection Agency Laboratory in Cincinnati.

C.B. Leib, who had faithfully served as a Company director for 31 years, retired in June 1985. Later that year, another director, L.W. Lane, Jr., chairman of the board of Lane Publishing Co. and *Sunset* magazine, resigned to accept an appointment from President Reagan as Ambassador to Australia and Nauru. He would be reelected to the Board in June 1990 following the end of his government assignment.

Then, in 1986, Robert Minge Brown would officially close his distinguished 33-year Cal Water career, retiring as a Company director. His personal commitment to excellence and integrity had guided the Company to the highest of standards. In his honor, the Board named him director emeritus.

Ralph D. Lindberg also retired as chief executive officer in 1986, concluding 29 years of Company service. His leadership tenure was held in high esteem and had brought the Company national recognition through his election as president of the National Association of Water Companies.

C.H. Stump became chief executive and continued in his post as president with Lindberg remaining chairman of the Board. Stump had begun his remarkable career with the Company in 1950 as a field employee in San Mateo, which is now part of the Bayshore District.

Jeptha A. Wade, Jr., ended his own distinguished Company career in July 1987, retiring as vice president and chief engineer. His 40-year tenure had contributed significantly to the success of Cal Water, earning him national recognition in the water industry. Wade also served as a member or chairman of many committees of the American Water Works Association and other professional organizations. David C. Heninger, who had joined the engineering staff in

1946, replaced him as chief engineer. In 1988, the board also elected two new officers, Kenneth J. Roed, director of corporate communications with 12 years service, as vice president, and Roberta Nelson as assistant secretary and director of personnel. Nelson had 34 years service with the Company in personnel and accounting.

The Company's financial strength and stature had reached a major milestone during the final years of the eighties. The annual stock dividend in 1987 had risen to $1.48 per share, or 6 percent over the prior year, the 20th consecutive year the dividend had been increased. The stock split 2 for 1 in October, the second such split in the previous four years. Annual operating revenue rose to a record $112,776,000 and earnings for the year increased 10 percent to $2.64 per share. It was the fifth consecutive increase in annual earnings. The Company's bond rating had been raised the previous year by Standard & Poor's Corporation from A+ to AA+ and by Moody's Investors Service, Inc. from A2 to Aa2. The Standard & Poor's rating was the highest given to any California utility, and in November of that same year, the Company was included in *Forbes* magazine's list of 200 best small companies in America with sales under $350 million.

On October 19, 1989, the San Francisco Bay area suffered its most destructive earthquake since 1906. Fortunately, less than one percent, or 750 Company customers, in the Bay Area experienced interruption of water service for no more than a 24-hour period. A letter of commendation was received from the Governor praising employees for their dedication to duty during the earthquake's aftermath.

With the Company's new leadership in place and its reputation growing within the utility and financial communities, California Water Service Company was prepared to step boldly into the century's final decade.

This early 1980s photograph of General Office ladies represents a total of more than 300 combined years of service to the Company. By 2004, all had retired except for Anita Paramo, seated, second from right, who is engineering executive secretary, with 53 years Company service. Seated, from left, Bobbie Nelson, Joy Tripoli, Mrs. Paramo and Mary Lou Caccamo; standing, from left, Lois Wiley, Marion Frasier, Bernice Raymond, Marguerite St. Aubin, Dorothy Shepard and Phyllis Lovoi.

Representatives on the Company's Utility Workers Union of America Council are shown at this early 1980s gathering. Seated, from left, Chris Carrasco (SLN), John Bertoglio (ELA), T. C. Dennis (ORO), Ed Hall, Utility Union regional director, and Tyrone Robinson (MPS). Back row, from left, Peter Akhotnikoff (PV), Peter Salazar (BK), Ken Huber (STK/ GO) Toni Ruggle (CH), Mike Jones, (PV/GO), Keith Wilson (BK), Jim Leven (ELA) and Mike Stevens (STK/GO).

Bobbie Nelson's retirement hi-jinks starring Gerry Feeney and Dino Coppe in a "Driving Miss Daisy" skit.

The Camys...a three-generation Cal Water family. Mike Camy, at left, Stockton district manager, who retired in March 2001, is shown with son, Doug, utility worker in Visalia. Mike's dad, Laurence Camy, was one of the Company's first employees in 1926.

From left, retirees Hal Emmerich, asst. secretary/asst. treasurer; Ken Kilby, construction superintendent; Les Saxe, corporate secretary.

Former district managers share a moment of fun to reminisce about times past covering well over 100 years of combined Company service. From left, Bob Lewis, Les Carlson, Barney Tumey and S.M. "Di" Martino.

More than 200 years of service is represented here by this Cal Water team, shown with spouses enjoying retirement party festivities. From left, seated, Clay Scofield, Myra Scofield, Dino Coppe, Pat Coppe. Back row, from left, Al Larson, Barney Tumey, Doris Tumey, Mary Palermo, Elsie Nahmens, Sam Palermo, Bill Nahmens, Dave Diamond.

Representing more than 160 years of Company service, front row, from left, Rose Zey and Ken Dow, Walt and Lea Delsigne, Leroy Palmer; back row, Bob and Martha Schuster, Bob and Judy White.

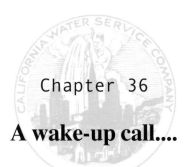

Chapter 36

A wake-up call....

As 1990 emerged, California was undergoing one of its severest droughts in recorded history. The dry period had commenced during 1987 and would continue for the next 5 1/2 years. In the spring of 1990, the San Francisco Water Department, the Company's water supplier for its Peninsula Districts, initiated mandatory water rationing for 84,000 customers. Subsequently, the California Public Utilities Commission authorized the Company to begin rationing in South San Francisco, San Carlos, San Mateo and Bear Gulch. Customers were required to reduce annual water use by 25 percent under threat of monetary penalties for exceeding their water allotments. At the same time, another wholesale supplier, the Santa Clara Valley Water District, also required the Company's Los Altos District customers to reduce water use by 20 percent.

As the drought continued into 1991, mandatory water rationing had become a way of life for customers in five more Cal Water districts. In the south, the Metropolitan Water District of Southern California initiated a 20-percent water use cutback affecting four districts — Hermosa-Redondo, East Los Angeles, Palos Verdes and Westlake. And in the Company's Stockton District, the area's wholesale supplier, the Stockton-East Water District, ordered a 20-percent reduction in customer water use. The severity of the drought was emphasized by the sobering fact that during most of 1991, approximately 58 percent or 207,000 of the Company's total customers were under water rationing.

Two months into 1991, it was announced that state reservoir supplies were down to 20 percent of average. Although groundwater tables were lower than normal during the year, there still remained substantial reserves in the underground aquifers that supplied Company districts. More than 500 wells in 16 districts were providing one-half of the Company's statewide supply to meet customer needs. With California's population growing by some 700,000 annually, five consecutive years of drought was sending a wake-up call to state and local planners. There was a critical demand for building consensus among water interests throughout California to meet future water supply needs.

During this period, the Company was an active participant in the State's call for a "Memorandum of Understanding" among 123 water agencies throughout California. Water purveyors were asked to support "Best Management Practices" designed to promote the efficient use of water. The Memorandum was signed by Cal Water and all participating agencies in ceremonies held in Sacramento in May 1991. Eight more difficult months followed before the drought finally broke.

At its meeting in April 1990, the Board of Directors elected Raymond H. Taylor as vice president for water quality and environmental affairs. He had been director of water quality for the Company since 1986. In July, Lester E. Saxe retired as secretary and was replaced by Helen Mary Kasley, formerly an associate attorney with the McCutchen law firm in San Francisco. Saxe's Company service totaled 28 years, including eight as secretary.

As 1990 was ending, the Company announced the sale of $20 million in 30-year first mortgage bonds to help finance the Company's proposed expansion program for 1991. It provided for construction of a 15,800-sq.-ft. engineering/water quality facility to be built at the General Office complex and extensive remodeling of existing office facilities. The project was scheduled for completion in the spring of 1992.

In June 1991, Ralph D. Lindberg stepped down as chairman of the Board and was replaced by C.H. Stump. Elected president was Donald L. Houck, who would become chief executive officer the following year upon Stump's retirement. Houck was a native of St. Louis, Missouri, and a 1955 engineering graduate of the University of Missouri at Columbia. He was an expert in public utility regulation, having served 17 years on the staff of the California Public Utilities Commission before joining the Company in 1977. During his tenure with Cal Water, Houck was responsible for overseeing regulatory affairs and rate-case filings that generated millions of dollars in rate relief.

New programs and projects were initiated during the early years of the decade, bringing further improvements to water quality and customer billing operations. The Company undertook a $1 million program to upgrade water treatment facilities in the Bear Gulch service area to meet new state and federal surface water regulations, thus enabling the District's treatment plant and reservoir to provide an additional surface water supply to customers.

In Bakersfield, Cal Water introduced a special catalytic carbon treatment process to remove the onerous odor of hydrogen sulfide (the rotten-egg smell common in coastal communities) detected at specific well sites. The program proved highly effective and a most popular treatment of the water supply in the Bakersfield District. The Company also increased efforts to remove volatile organic chemicals (VOCs) from the underground aquifers in Chico through a joint venture with the State Department of Health Services. The cost-sharing project was a milestone in government and private cooperation, incorporating a granular-activated carbon system for the removal of the contaminant PCE. Finally, in its sustaining effort to ensure compliance with federal and state bacteriological standards, Company sanitary engineers began the installation of chlorinators on all wells throughout the state.

Cal Water received national recognition in 1991 for a unique program initiated by Raymond Worrell in data processing to improve efficiency in customer billing. Company-designed work stations were installed for processing incoming customer bills, incorporating innovative equipment that increased productivity by as much as 50 to 80 percent. The program received first-place honors in the Innovative Management competition sponsored by the National Association of Water Companies. Within two years, Worrell and his department would once again receive NAWC's top honors, this time for innovations in Company mailing procedures, which had also been nationally recognized by the U.S. Postal Service.

By the end of 1991, total customers for the year had increased by 4,300, including 600 new services through the acquisition of the Goshen water system. Its operations were integrated with the Company's Visalia District.

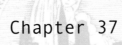

Chapter 37

Stepping into the future...

Parker Robinson was pleased when he toured Cal Water's new engineering/water quality building on its opening during the spring of 1992. As he inspected the new facilities, the retired assistant chief engineer reminisced back 20 years when he had first presented his case to management for moving aggressively into the computer age. Instead of one computer serving the entire department, Robinson found more than 40 now meeting the individual requirements of all engineers, draftsmen, technicians and secretaries.

The new 15,800-sq.-ft. facility had transformed Cal Water's engineering and water quality programs into elaborate computerized operations, bringing reality to Robinson's past dreams. The building was part of the first expansion/remodeling program undertaken at the General Office since 1973, when facilities for information systems had been constructed.

The $3.8-million engineering and water quality complex was among the most technically advanced facilities to be built in the water service industry. Within the 10,000-sq.-ft. area designated for engineering, draftsmen would now perform much of their mapping work via computers. Engineers had access to the latest in computer technology, including the use of scanners to copy developer plans, thus enabling a more efficient process in the design of water systems. Through the department's increased network capabilities, engineers could now send water system designs electronically to the districts for input from developers and supervisors. Computerization of the engineering function also brought greater efficiency in creating budgets for future construction and maintenance programs.

The water quality laboratory occupied 5,800 sq. ft. in the new building and featured some of the industry's most technically advanced testing equipment. Separate areas of the laboratory were devoted to bacteriological analyses and testing for organic and inorganic chemicals. The laboratory in San Jose had long been regarded as one of the State's finest water testing operations. However, the new facility with its "state-of-the-art" equipment advanced Cal Water's water quality program to an even higher level of sophistication. It would permit the Company to address the growing demands of government regulations in water quality monitoring.

The 1992 expansion/remodeling program also called for the development of a media center and remodeling of facilities serving information systems, human resources, accounting, stores, purchasing and the employee lunch room.

In the late fall of that year, Cal Water announced plans to acquire the Del Este Water Company in Modesto, California, through a stock purchase agreement. However, the Company chose to nullify the proposed acquisition when it was determined it would precipitate condemnation action by the city.

C.H. "Bud" Stump stepped down as chief executive officer in May 1992, upon reaching the mandatory retirement age, but continued to serve as chairman, with Donald L. Houck, president and chief operating officer, replacing him as chief executive. Houck had been with the Company since 1977, serving 15 years as vice president of regulatory affairs.

Water agencies throughout California welcomed the deluge of storms that struck the State during the winter of 1992-1993. It brought a dramatic end to the 5 1/2-year drought, the longest dry period in California during the past 60 years. By February of 1993,. it was predicted that the State's 155 reservoirs would be at near or full capacity by the end of the spring runoff season with the Sierra snow-pack reaching 200 percent of normal capacity.

Mandatory rationing was eliminated in those districts most severely affected by the drought, but customers statewide were urged to continue practicing conservation on a voluntary basis. In some districts it was noted that undergroundwater tables had not fully recovered from the effects of the drought. And state water officials warned that California would have long-term water supply problems as growth continued at an accelerated pace. Only customers in the Salinas Valley would be required to maintain a 15-percent voluntary reduction in water use to comply with a government ordinance. The county's Water Resources Agency had requested purveyors adopt water use restrictions as one step toward protecting the Valley's underground aquifer from salt water intrusion from Monterey Bay.

In September 1993, Robert J. Glazer, M.D. retired from the Cal Water Board, ending 21 years of distinguished service. His vacancy was filled with the election of Edward D. Harris, Jr., M.D., professor of medicine and chairman of the Department of Medicine, Stanford University Medical Center.

Fred L. Dodge, who had lived and shaped so much of the history of Cal Water, died in 1993 during his 94th year. The former president, who had joined the Company as manager of the East Los Angeles District in 1927, retired in 1965. He was affiliated with Cal Water for 57 years, including 27 years as a director and director emeritus. His tenure has been the longest of any Company employee.

Dodge's passing would be followed within a year by the death of another highly respected Company leader, Robert Minge Brown. In its

1994 annual report, Cal Water paid a fitting tribute to its former chief executive and legal counsel:

"It is hard to imagine the Company without Bob...his mix of humor, business acumen, legal knowledge and the highest ethical standards provided the Company with considered and welcome guidance through good times and bad. His counsel will be sorely missed."

Incredibly, one year after being challenged by one of its longest periods of drought, California again was threatened by the fickle nature of its weather patterns. The State's Department of Water Resources announced that the 1993-94 water season had been the fourth driest on record, and as a consequence, the agency was declaring a "drought watch" for the State to answer the threat of another water-short year. The Company continued its emphasis on customer conservation and there was no call for rationing in any district. Fortunately, the dry period would be short-lived as a series of winter storms began in November of 1994 and continued unabated throughout the winter months, ending the State's "drought watch" warning.

A major earthquake struck southern California on Jan. 17, 1994, in the Northridge section of San Fernando Valley. The surrounding area was one in which Cal Water provided service to more than a quarter of a million people. Although there was widespread devastation, only minor damage was caused at Cal Water facilities. However, to assist the more affected communities, service crews from Visalia and Bakersfield were dispatched to the cities hardest hit by the quake to help restore water service.

Cal Water reached another milestone as a publicly held Company when its common stock began trading on the New York Stock Exchange on April 29, 1994, under the symbol "CWT." The Company had previously traded on the NASDAQ National Market with 5,688,754 shares of common stock held by approximately 5,500 shareholders as of Dec. 31, 1993. The sale of 550,000 additional shares of common stock would be held in September 1994, marking the first time the Company had sold common stock since the 1950s.

In 1994, the Company began to move aggressively into a program that provided various contract services to municipal and other government agencies. It would also announce plans to seek opportunities for full-service operating and management agreements with municipal-owned water systems. Agreements were signed with the Central and West Basin Municipal Water Districts in Los Angeles for the operation and maintenance of the Districts' recycled water distribution systems. The Central Basin agreement had been the first of its kind for the Company and called for the operation of the District's Rio Hondo Recycled Water System. Up to 15,000 acre feet of reclaimed water would be produced from the Rio Hondo system for irrigation and industrial use. The recycled supply would also be available for resale by the Company to customers in East Los Angeles for industrial processed water and for irrigating parks, green belts, golf courses and school playing fields. Municipal contracts were signed in three districts to include other city utility services as part of the Company's monthly water bill. In King City and Willows, customer water bills included city sewer charges, and in Visalia, the water bill included the charge for city sewer and refuse services.

Donald L. Houck
*President and Chief Executive
Officer from 1992 to 1996.
An expert in water utility
regulation, he served two
terms as president of the
California Water Association.*

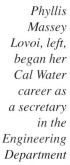

*Phyllis
Massey
Lovoi, left,
began her
Cal Water
career as
a secretary
in the
Engineering
Department
in September 1945, one month following the end of World War II. She
enjoys a special moment here at her retirement party in June of 1991
with her replacement, Executive Secretary Dolores Wriglesworth.*

In the spring of 1992, construction was completed on the 15,800-sq.-ft. water quality/ engineering building at the Company's headquarters in San Jose. The complex and its equipment continues today to be recognized among the most technically advanced facilities within the water utility industry. The top photograph shows Anita Paramo, engineering executive secretary, and Senior Engineering Assistant Fred Rios in foreground, and at far right, Senior Engineering Assistant Ed Harr. Mrs. Paramo celebrated her 53rd year at Cal Water in 2004!

Changing with the times...

"The design of Company well stations, commonly referred to as pump houses, has changed drastically over the years. The very early designs called for the construction of the masonry buildings built during the twenties and thirties. They had a recessed pump pit outside and built-in planter boxes which were unique for the period. The masonry pump station design was followed by wood-framed stucco buildings and then metal buildings, usually constructed by Steelox or Butler. These were followed by the wood-framed 'cottage-type' well stations which were popular in the forties and fifties. They originally had cedar shingle roofing, but later replaced with asphalt shingles, in neighborhoods where appropriate, to allow for better fire protection and cost savings. During more recent times, Company wells in residential neighborhoods have been housed in attractively designed structures built with concrete block and slump stone."

Ralph Steiber, retired, asst. chief engineer; 37 years service

Chapter 38

A feeling of family,
a very special relationship...

On Nov. 30, 1994, L.W. "Bill" Lane, Jr., former president and publisher of *Sunset* magazine and Ambassador to Australia and Nauru, retired as a Company director after 23 years of distinguished service. Ambassador Lane had first joined the Board in 1967, but his service was interrupted during the eighties when President Reagan chose him for the Australian diplomatic post. The year he retired from the Board, he received the "1994 Conservationist of the Year Award" from the National Parks and Conservation Association. Several years after his retirement, Ambassador Lane would comment:

"I have to say that my service with Cal Water probably was the most enjoyable Board relationship. There was the camaraderie of the Board, as well as the subject material that was always dear to my heart. It just was a very, very fine relationship over the years. While Cal Water was not a 'family' in the same way as the Lane Publishing was, you certainly had the feeling of family and that was a very special relationship. The Company's emphasis on its quality of customer service was a fact that had always appealed to me. Cal Water had a good employee relationship that I felt was synergistic with the various districts of the Company. That was always the paramount goal — to indoctrinate the service people as well as upgrading the quality of the hardware. The fact that Cal Water was dedicated to that quality of service reflected throughout the whole organization, through to the stockholders and the investment community."

Ambassador Lane was replaced on the Board by the election of Linda Randall Meier, who at the time was chair of the Stanford University Hospital Board of Directors and currently serves as a Board member of the Comerica Bank-California. In another Board matter during 1994, Roscoe Moss, Jr., who had served as a director since 1982, resigned and was replaced by J.W. Weinhardt, president and chief executive of SJW Corp. In recognition of his service, the Board commended Moss for his commitment to Cal Water as a major shareholder and for *"his dedication to upholding the Company's reputation for excellence, integrity and professionalism."*

Several executive appointments were also announced during the year with the election of Gerald F. Feeney to vice president, chief financial officer and treasurer; Raymond H. Taylor, to vice president of water quality and environmental affairs; James L. Good, to vice president of corporate communications and marketing; and Calvin L. Breed, to controller and assistant secretary and assistant treasurer. Retiring was Harold C. Ulrich, who had served the Company with great distinction over a 32-year career, first as controller and later as vice president, chief financial officer and treasurer. Good, who replaced Kenneth J. Roed, vice president of corporate communications with 18 years service, was previously director of congressional relations for the National Association of Water Companies. Feeney had served as Company controller and Taylor as director of water quality. Breed was formerly treasurer of TCI International, a defense contractor.

Chapter 39

"Like a thunderbolt from the sky..."

It was a warm, sunny day back in May of 1976 when Ralph Lindberg and Robert Minge Brown made their 80-mile drive to Stockton. Robert W. Foy remembers their visit well:

"I was president of the Chamber of Commerce at the time, and I was scheduled to meet and have lunch with two Company executives from San Jose. Bob Lewis, Cal Water's Stockton manager, had arranged a luncheon, explaining that the visitors wanted to know about the present-day economy in our City just to be better informed. Since I was the Chamber president, Lewis explained they thought I would be the best one to see. A week after our luncheon, Ralph Lindberg called me and said, 'Well, you made it! We would like to have you join the Cal Water Board.'

"That came like a thunderbolt from the sky! They had given me no idea whatsoever that our luncheon meeting had another purpose. I knew it was a very, very wonderful Company and I was glad to become a part of it." Little did Foy realize at the time, that nearly two decades later he would once again be chosen — this time, to become chairman of the Board of California Water Service Company.

Lindberg and Brown would soon realize at the time of their first meeting with Foy that not only were they being introduced to a very well-respected, successful and honored member of the Stockton community, his credentials would show he had a great deal more to offer.

A fourth-generation Californian, Foy was born in San Francisco in 1936 and was graduated from San Jose State University with a bachelor of science degree in business and industrial management. He was elected the outstanding male graduate of his Class of 1959, receiving University Distinction and College of Business Honors. His alma mater would later honor him as recipient of the University's prestigious 1981 College of Business Distinguished Alumnus Award.

Following his graduation and military service as an officer in the U.S. Army, he worked for several years with the Continental Can Co., traveling extensively throughout the United States. Foy had already risen to purchasing agent when he decided to leave Continental, settling in Stockton where he joined the Pacific Storage Company. In 1977, he was elected president and CEO of Pacific Storage, the second oldest and third largest Bekins Moving and Storage agent in the United States with offices in Stockton, San Jose, Sacramento, Modesto, Merced, Vallejo and Auburn. He served as head of Pacific Storage until 1995 and continues today as a partner and member of its Board of Directors. Throughout his career, Foy has been a volunteer and leader for scores of business, community and professional organizations.*

On Jan. 1, 1996, Foy began his new challenge as chairman of the Board of California Water Service Company, replacing C. H. "Bud" Stump, who was retiring. Throughout his 45-year career, Stump had been closely involved with Company personnel matters. It was his personal interaction with employees and his positive, empathetic and consistent manner that had won him their respect and admiration. His dedication to promoting and achieving excellence in customer service

*In addition to serving as president of the Stockton Chamber, his other activities included president of the San Joaquin County United Way; president of the California Moving and Storage Association; chairman of the Bekins Van Lines Company Agency Advisory Council; chairman of the board of the National Moving & Storage Association; chairman of the Board of Commissioners of the Stockton Port District; president of the Stockton Yosemite Club; chairman of the Board of Trustees of St. Joseph's Medical Center of Stockton; chairman of the Advisory Board of the Eberhardt School of Business at the University of Pacific; and Clerk of the Vestry of St. John's Episcopal Church of Stockton.

had been unequaled among those with whom he served.

Donald L. Houck, the Company's chief executive officer since 1992, followed Stump in retirement on Jan. 31, 1996. He was well-known and respected throughout the water utility industry, serving as a director of the National Association of Water Companies and two terms as president of the California Water Association (CWA). His leadership within CWA helped build a positive working relationship between California's private water utilities and the state legislature.

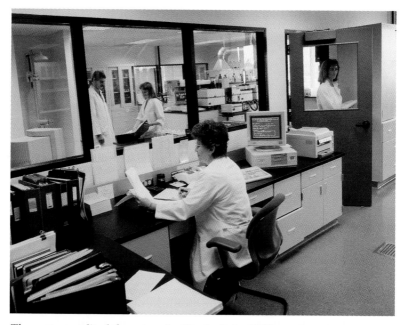

The water quality laboratory facility built in 1992 continues to ensure the quality of water delivered to all service areas is meeting the ever-increasing demands of federal and state standards. Shown here in this early-nineties photograph were staff members, from left, Gary Falling, Kelly Scoffone-O'Dea, Veronica Simion and Lori Preston.

Chapter 40

Searching for the "perfect fit"...

W hen the directors of Cal Water first approached Foy in the fall of 1995 regarding the chairmanship, he was also asked to head the search committee to find the person who would be the next president and chief executive officer. A big task lay ahead.

The committee sought a uniquely balanced individual. One, of course, who was highly qualified and experienced to lead the Company aggressively and successfully. But equally important, a leader who possessed the ability to understand, respect and retain the essence of Cal Water and its culture. There was a heritage to preserve. Additionally, the new leader would be one who would appreciate and maintain the "one team" concept. An individual who would instill a vibrant entrepreneurial spirit among all employees to help the Company grow. After a nationwide search and all candidates carefully considered, Foy said there was no doubt as to the committee's choice. All agreed that Peter C. Nelson "was the perfect fit for the job."

As fortune would have it, Nelson had just recently left his position as vice president-division operations for Pacific Gas & Electric Company in the fall of 1995 to pursue other interests. He had been employed by PG&E since 1971, assigned to various positions in engineering, construction management, diversification planning, finance, operations and general management. A native of Ross, California, Nelson was a 1971 graduate of the University of California at Davis with a bachelor of science degree in mechanical engineering.

He earned an M.B.A. from the University of Massachusetts, Amherst in 1976.

Changes were taking place rapidly within the water utility industry at the time Nelson took command on Feb. 1, 1996. His challenge was to make the Company grow in an increasingly competitive environment, driven by the consolidation of the country's water utilities, by competition from European companies entering the U.S. utility market and by increasingly stringent federal and state water quality standards.

Five years into Nelson's Cal Water tenure, one member of the original executive search committee would extend high marks:

"It has been a difficult time with so many changes going on in the Company and in the industry. Pete has been exactly the right person to lead that change and meet our new challenges. He is a highly ethical person and that is so important for Cal Water because that is what our Company has stood for. He has a broad knowledge of so many areas and can take a complicated issue and put it into simple terms that everyone understands. He has an appreciation for how important the employee is to the Company. He doesn't make emotional decisions, but bases them on logic and care. He understands the value of customers and how we need to respond to their needs. And finally, he appreciates and understands the shareholders and what they need from us."

Robert W. Foy
Chairman of the Board 1996-
A member of the Cal Water
Board of Directors since
1977, his leadership provides
a valuable link to the
Company's contributions of
the past with the innovations
and goals of present day.

Peter C. Nelson
President and Chief Executive
Officer 1996-
Through his experience
and leadership in the utility
field, he would bring a
dynamic new vision and focus
to California Water Service,
building upon the Company's
reputation for high standards
and professionalism.

Chapter 41

One-on-one with the boss...

"*It was a day not easy to forget,*" explained Gene Myers, Cal Water's veteran serviceman/storekeeper. "*It was February 1996 and as a field worker in the Hermosa-Redondo District, I had been given the task that morning of 'showing the ropes' on customer service calls to one of the Company's newest employees.*" But, of course, Myers knew that his charge for that day was no ordinary 'new hire.' "*He was the boss,*" Myers explained, "*Cal Water's new CEO and president.*"

Within a few months of taking command on Feb. 1, 1996, Pete Nelson would be no stranger to Gene Myers nor to Cal Water's 630 employees statewide. During his first 90 days on the job, Nelson had made it a top priority to meet and exchange questions and answers with every employee, usually in small groups. He made service calls, read meters, visited the commercial offices, always asking questions and seeking input on what improvements should be made.

In recalling his own experience with Nelson that day in 1996, Myers said the CEO showed real interest in learning what customer service was all about at Cal Water. "*As for myself,*" Myers said, "*I felt genuinely honored that I had the opportunity to give him my 'take' on dealing with customers. It was quite an experience.*

"*In terms of going 'one-on-one' with the CEO, even if only for a few hours that morning, I discovered he was a regular guy...he was the boss, of course...but at the same time, someone easy to know.*

"*Before I had hired on at the Company in 1976, I had been a rough kid, quitting school early, holding jobs that really had no future. Being 27 years old at the time, I was aware of what was out there in terms of jobs for someone like myself... young with limited experience who had left school early. But I was given a chance. I knew from the very beginning that Cal Water would be my career and I intended to make the most of it. I had an opportunity to share some of this that day with Pete."*

On doing what is right...

"It's much easier for us to do the right thing from the beginning rather than wait for something wrong to happen and then you have a black mark against you. And that's the way Cal Water works. ***We have always put service and employees before money.*** *We have taken heat when we have raised rates and sometimes the smaller systems have had water costing more because the systems are more costly to serve. And we have had to take some pretty good heat in a couple of our systems when we have done that. But they never ever say anything bad about the service. As a result, we have the fewest customer complaints of any major water company."*

**Stan Ferraro, vice president, regulatory matters 2004,
California Water Service Company**

Chapter 42

A "win-win" situation...

At the time Nelson assumed leadership of the Company, Cal Water had already embraced a business concept known as public-private partnerships. It was a program in which Cal Water entered into contracts with governmental agencies to perform services allied to the Company's utility business. One such significant contract, ironically, came into being on Nelson's very first day as chief executive. The City of Hawthorne in Los Angeles County announced that the Cal Water was the winner of a competitive bidding auction for a 15-year lease to operate and manage the City's 6,000 customer municipal water system.

As Nelson noted at the time, the private-public partnership was believed to be the first of its kind in California and a "win-win" situation for both the City and the Company. Under terms of the contract, Cal Water had agreed to an up-front cash payment of $6,525,000 to the City in addition to an annual lease payment of $100,000. The Company also agreed to make all necessary capital improvements to the system, subject to approval by the City Council. Cal Water, in turn, would receive all system revenues, estimated to average more than $4 million annually for the term of the contract. Water rates would be set at the same level as those of the Company's adjacent Hermosa-Redondo District, subject to approval by the Hawthorne City Council. The Hawthorne lease arrangement brought a significant increase in the Company's unregulated business activity, which is not subject to control by the State's Public Utilities Commission. By the end of 1996, the Company already had 13 unregulated service contracts, including the 15-year Hawthorne lease. Among these were agreements to operate and maintain city-owned water utilities serving 23,500 customers in Bakersfield, Commerce and Montebello. In Menlo Park, the Company had an operating agreement calling for contract services for meter reading, billing and customer service. In four cities — Marysville, Willows, King City and Torrance — Cal Water had billing service contracts that called for city sewer charges to be part of the Company's monthly water bill. Similar billing contracts were in effect in Visalia for refuse and sewer services, and in Chico, for both household hazardous waste and sewer services. Finally, ongoing agreements were in effect with the Central and West Basin Municipal Water Districts in Los Angeles for the operation and maintenance of the Districts' recycled water distribution systems.

Company leaders joined in the celebration at the New York Stock Exchange on Nov. 23, 1998, at the closing bell on a day the Dow Jones average

reached an all-time high. Participants were, from left, Gerry Feeney, vice president and chief financial officer; Anita Mazur, Company consultant; William Johnson, president of the NYSE; Robert Foy, CWS chairman of the Board; Peter Nelson, CWS president and chief executive officer; and Calvin Breed, controller.

Ambassador L. W. ("Bill") Lane, Jr.
An ardent Cal Water supporter, he served on the Board of Directors for 23 years, retiring in 1994.

Chapter 43

Positioning the team...

Six months into his presidency, Pete Nelson had in place a strong executive team, finalized with the election of four officers from the employee ranks with a total of 99 years of combined Company service. They included three new vice presidents: Robert R. Guzzetta, engineering and water quality; Christine L. McFarlane, human resources; and Raymond L. Worrell, information systems. And Paul G. Ekstrom was named corporate secretary. The four new officers had made major contributions to the Company in their respective areas.

Guzzetta had been with the Company since 1977 and had served as chief engineer since 1988. A graduate of San Jose State University with bachelor and master's degrees in engineering, he lead the department to the present-day period of "computer engineering," overseeing the construction of the new engineering/water quality building complex in 1992.

McFarlane had been director of human resources since 1991 and held a variety of administrative positions during her 28-year career. In 1994, she was nominated for the prestigious YWCA Tribute to Woman and Industry Award.

Worrell had been director of Information Systems since 1991 and an employee for 29 years, playing a major role in converting the Company's billing program from mechanical operations to its various stages of data processing. He had been nationally recognized for his innovations in both in-house mailing procedures and in customer billing methods that had revolutionized remittance processing.

Ekstrom had started with the Company in 1972 as a utility worker and pump operator in the South San Francisco District, rising to become manager of the Livermore District. This was followed by his appointment as operations coordinator for the entire Company, a position he held prior to being named corporate secretary.

Also part of Nelson's executive team were five seasoned officers who were experts in their fields. Gerald F. Feeney, vice president, treasurer and chief financial officer, was a certified public accountant and had been in his present position since Jan. 1, 1995. A graduate of San Jose State University, he was Company controller for 18 years and had been an account executive with Peat, Marwick, Mitchell & Co.

Francis S. "Stan" Ferraro, vice president for regulatory matters, served as an administrative law judge for the California Public Utilities Commission and had been on the Commission staff for 16 years prior to his affiliation with Cal Water in 1989. He held a civil engineering degree from Merrimack College.

Ray Taylor, vice president of operations, joined the Company in 1982, and had been director of water quality and environmental affairs since 1986. He was selected to head operations in 1995. Before joining the Company, Taylor worked 17 years for the U.S. Environmental Protection Agency in water research and treatment and held a bachelor's degree from Miami University (Ohio) and a master's in environmental engineering from the University of Cincinnati.

James L. Good had been vice president of corporate communications and marketing since 1995. He was previously employed as director of congressional relations for the National Association of Water Companies and as deputy legislative director for U. S. Senator Harry Reid of Nevada. He was a graduate of Cornell University with a bachelor's degree in government.

John S. Simpson, assistant corporate secretary and manager of new business, had risen from the Company's ranks, starting as a temporary summer relief worker in 1964 in the Los Altos Suburban District. Before he was assigned to the General Office in 1984, Simpson had literally "run the gamut" in service to the Company. This included work as meter reader, collector, pump operator, clerk, assistant bookkeeper, manager of the Company's central billing operations, Stockton office manager and local manager in Marysville.

Calvin L. Breed, controller, assistant secretary and assistant treasurer, had been with the Company since 1994. He served previously as treasurer of TCI International, Inc., a manufacturer of high-frequency communications equipment and as a CPA with Arthur Andersen & Co. He held a bachelor's degree in business administration from California Polytechnic State University, San Luis Obispo.

The Board of Directors said farewell to another of its longtime and respected members on Nov. 30, 1996, with the retirement of William E. Ayer, who had been a Company director for 23 years. Elected to fill the Board vacancy was Richard P. Magnuson, a general partner of Menlo Ventures, a venture capital firm capitalized at more than $460 million. A member of the California State Bar, Magnuson was a graduate of Stanford University with a bachelor's degree in economics. He also held M.B.A. and J.D. degrees from the Stanford Graduate School of Business and Stanford Law School.

During 1996, the Company was saddened by the death of Ralph D. Lindberg, one of the outstanding leaders from the Company's past. He had served as treasurer, vice president, president, chief executive officer and chairman in his 39-year Cal Water career. During his leadership, the Company grew from 243,000 customers in 1966 to 358,000 in 1991, while gross revenue increased from $20,760,000 to $127,176,000.

Chapter 44

From utility to holding company...

At the Nov. 20, 1996, Board meeting, directors took a dramatic first step toward developing new growth opportunities and challenges for the Company. A resolution was passed unanimously calling for the formation of a holding company, the California Water Service Group. Chairman Robert Foy announced at the time that the Board's action would position Cal Water to become a leader in both traditional and innovative utility services. In years past, most of Cal Water's revenue was derived from operating water systems that were owned by the Company and regulated by the California Public Utilities Commission. However, it was believed that many revenue-producing opportunities could involve partnerships with governmental agencies, falling outside traditional regulatory practice. A case in point was the innovative long-term lease of the City of Hawthorne's water system signed early in the year, together with previously signed billing contracts with California cities.

Cal Water's corporate structure at the time gave the CPUC jurisdiction over the Company's unregulated operations such as the Hawthorne lease. Under a holding company structure, unregulated subsidiary services could be developed while not falling under the authority of the CPUC. It would provide financing flexibility and eliminate uncertainty in the allocation of costs between regulated and unregulated business operations. Benefits could also flow to existing customers by facilitating growth and providing a larger customer base to spread fixed costs of operations.

The Board felt that the legal and regulatory requirements needed to form the holding company could be completed in time for shareholder consideration and vote at the April 1997 annual meeting. In the meantime, the Company was actively pursuing new business through CWS Utility Services, its unregulated service subsidiary. It was organized to offer water companies, municipalities and other governmental agencies a complete range of utility services. These included meter reading, billing, leak detection, engineering services, water treatment,water testing, recycled water operations and design, and waste-water operations. Staffing and management of the program would be performed by Cal Water personnel. Through CWS Utility Services, municipalities were presented with a variety of water-service options that could provide the cities a new and secure source of revenue. The Company felt that such partnerships would be especially appealing once the municipality understood that the city would retain control over water rates, service standards and system improvements.

Before the Company's new leadership team would end its first year at the helm, it would embark upon yet another ambitious program — one dedicated to excelling in meeting the needs of those who are served.

It began with a uniquely designed process known as the "Voice of the Customer" through which the view of hundreds of Company customers throughout California were captured via personal interviews, small focus groups and surveys, all designed to identify needs and concerns.

The thoroughness and extent of the undertaking quite possibly was a first within the water utility industry. Amazingly, 72 areas were identified in which customers expressed specific needs and concerns regarding water utility service. With data in hand, Vice President Paul Ekstrom and Ed Sliger, director of customer service, led a company-wide team to implement a four-step process which would:

(1) Identify and prioritize the needs expressed by customers,

(2) Look within the Company to identify and measure specific areas — activities, tasks or results — that would predict a customer receiving excellent service,

(3) Conduct follow-up surveys to check on the results of the Company's efforts to deliver excellent service and

(4) Ensure that a continuous improvement process was in place to sustain and enhance the customer service program.

It was an innovative approach to reinforce the Company's on-going commitment to excellence in customer service.

On the legislative front, a new federal law was adopted during 1996 that was expected to favor new business growth for investor-owned water utilities. The law repealed the federal tax on developers' up-front contributions in aid of construction (CIAC) to fund new subdivision water facilities. As a result, the cost of developer-funded projects would be reduced by approximately 30 percent.

It had been a landmark year for Cal Water and its new leadership. Change was indeed under way and a new vision had been created within the Company which was dedicated to being *the* leader in providing communities and customers with traditional and innovative utility services.

Chapter 45

Investing in our core business...

A robust financial summary would greet directors at their first meeting in January of 1997. Chairman Foy announced that 1996 had been a banner period for the Company as earnings and revenue reached record levels. Net income had passed $19 million with earnings rising 29 percent to $3.01 per share on revenue of $182,764,000.

With the strong financial performance came word that once again the dividend would be increased, this time for the 30th consecutive year. Further, it was announced that a two-for-one stock split would take place in conjunction with the Company's most significant under-taking in recent years, the creation of the holding company.

Having received approval from both the Company's shareholders and the California Public Utilities Commission, the California Water Service Group (Group) officially came into being on Dec. 31, 1997. The Group would have two operating subsidiaries — California Water Service Company (Cal Water) and CWS Utility Services (CWSUS). Its regulated utility operations would be conducted through Cal Water and non-regulated services through CWS Utility Services.

Common stock shareholders of California Water Service Company automatically became common stock shareholders in the Group on a two-for-one basis and listing on the New York Stock Exchange would continue under the symbol "CWT." The preferred shareholders of California Water Service Company became preferred shareholders of the holding company on a one-for-one basis, but would have voting

197

rights doubled.

With the Group now officially in place, Foy and Nelson explained that the new operating structure provided the Company the flexibility needed to remain competitive in the new century. At the same time, they said, it was important for the Company to provide shareholders with a higher return than what was traditionally expected from a utility. *"The holding company,"* they said in a letter to shareholders, *"will help us reach this goal by giving us greater flexibility to invest in opportunities not regulated by the California Public Utilities Commission. Not shopping malls and financial derivatives, but conservative investments in our core business — water utilities and related services."*

Formation of the holding company was just one of several highlights of 1997. An important change in California state law during the year provided the Company an opportunity for greater growth through acquisitions of private water utilities. Senate Bill 1268 would enable Cal Water to purchase a water company and still earn a fair rate of return for service to its new customers. Water rates would be based upon either the purchase price or upon replacement cost (net) less depreciation, whichever was lower. The new law thus allowed fair rates to be established, and Cal Water would now have greater incentive to invest in undercapitalized water systems which had been challenged financially to meet new water quality standards and maintain up-to-date facilities.

In another "first" for the Company, Cal Water was chosen to design, construct, operate, maintain and finance a water system in the foothills north of the City of Vacaville. The concept, from start to finish, was created by Cal Water personnel for what was believed to be the first new water district established in California during the past 25 years. The contract was awarded by the rural North Vacaville

Water District to provide water utility service to a developing, unincorporated area of Solano County.

Several major personnel matters also took place during 1997:

— Edwin E. van Bronkhorst, a distinguished and honored member of the Board of Directors, retired after 13 years of service. A trustee and treasurer of the David and Lucille Packard Foundation, van Bronkhorst had joined the Cal Water Board after his retirement as senior vice president, chief financial officer and treasurer of Hewlett-Packard Corp.

— Michael J. Rossi was named chief engineer, the ninth in a line of distinguished and dedicated engineers who have served in that position since the Company's founding. During his 20-year tenure with Cal Water, Rossi had played a major role in planning and executing the Company's annual construction budget, now totaling $28 million.

— The California-Nevada Section of the American Water Works Association awarded Company Vice President Raymond Taylor its prestigious 1997 George Warren Fuller Award for his outstanding service and leadership in the water supply field. It was the second year in a row that a Company representative was so honored. In 1996, Charles Nena, Cal Water's cross-connection manager, won the award for his service in the cross-connection field. In years past, the Fuller Award had also been bestowed upon Cal Water's Jack Rossum and George Adrian, both former directors of the Company's water quality program. In 2000, the Fuller Award would be bestowed upon yet another Cal Water staffer, Chet Auckly, the Company's current director of water quality and environmental affairs.

Chapter 46

"We pay you to dig...
We don't pay you to think!"

Vice President and Corporate Secretary Paul Ekstrom can still hear those words ringing in his ears when he thinks back nearly 30 years. Employed by the Company as a temporary field worker, he was down in a hole, digging ditches. Ekstrom had mistakenly presumed that his supervisor would be receptive to his suggestion... *"I think I have an idea for a better way to do this job."*

"Today," explains Christine McFarlane, vice president of human resources, *"the employee is paid not only to 'dig' but also to think and to contribute in all kinds of ways to help improve the Company and its operations. Leadership practices of companies during earlier decades reflected a command-and-control management style, always telling employees what to do and how to do it. By contrast, present day practice calls for supervisors and managers to coach and lead. One reason for the change is that our leaders are no longer the sole keepers of knowledge. Thanks to the new technology of today, knowledge is basically available to all, and thus allows us to contribute more effectively to our companies."*

During the nineties, a new approach to doing business was initiated at Cal Water known as Continuous Improvement, which in effect was a well-defined, structured, Company-wide process that focused on customer service, operating efficiency and developing the unrealized potential and contribution of every employee. Essentially, it was now every employee's responsibility to employ his or her talents and energy to improve service to customers and run an efficient operation.

"When we first adopted the concept," McFarlane says, *"we did so as a way to help our employees become more focused on serving the customer and working together as a team. When Pete Nelson became Company CEO, he totally embraced this approach to business and the involvement of every employee in the Company. Without his support and active participation, our program would not have enjoyed its present success."*

Continuous Improvement has been headed by McFarlane and Raymond Taylor, who is in charge of operations. The effort begins with Cal Water employees meeting together periodically to "brainstorm" ideas that could improve Company operations and service to the customer. The employees then select the ideas that they wish to develop. After a more detailed study, an employee team makes a formal business case presentation of its recommended improvements to a decision-making team of Company officers and General Office managers for consideration. Following approval, the team implements the improvements and checks to make sure the results are achieved.

The approach is unique in that every employee receives countless hours of training in how to identify, analyze and improve a business process; the employees closest to the work choose the areas to improve; and every employee performs public speaking every 90 days in presenting a business case to a high-level executive team, with his or her peers in the audience.

According to Taylor, widespread use of cellular phones was just one of many employee-generated ideas that have been adopted as a result of Continuous Improvement. An employee team presentation had effectively demonstrated how customer service, field emergencies and other Company business could be improved substantially, simply through a more extensive use of cellular phones. *"As a result,"* Taylor says, *"today every supervisor and most field workers are provided cell phones to permit instant communications.*

"Continuous Improvement has accomplished a great deal, and the results are truly dramatic. It has really changed the way we are doing business and serving our customers."

One important project that has generated areas to improve is the Company's "Voice of the Customer" program, which identifies through extensive research with Cal Water customers — in person and in small focus groups — the needs and concerns of residential customers. *"As a result, we have been told,"* Taylor explains, *"that the customer's number one concern is water quality. Consequently, in every district, at least one of our subjects for discussion deals with improving water quality. In the past, district staff would say, 'Why can't the General Office fix or solve this problem?' Today, district personnel are asked to become more involved by taking an active role in solving their own problems. So now the matter becomes the responsibility of every employee, not just the people at the General Office. And the ideas presented by the employees actually on the scene, more often than not, provide the best solution."*

Kent Adney was named Continuous Improvement manager in 2004.

Chapter 47

"Be all that you can be..."

From a Company standpoint, Continuous Improvement has indeed brought important benefits, many of which have affected the bottom line. Yet according to veteran Chico District staffer Vicky Mount, it has also brought significant personal pluses to those employees willing to embrace the program to its fullest extent. The well-known recruitment slogan, *"Be All That You Can Be,"* might best express the thoughts of Mount when she explains how Continuous Improvement, combined with other Company activities, has made a big impact on her work at Cal Water.

"Throughout my Company career, I've been encouraged, I've been 'stretched,' I've been constantly reminded by my supervisors that I could be and do more than I ever thought possible." During her 17-year Cal Water career, Mount has served as a clerk, pump operator, water treatment operator, water distribution operator, meter reader, locator and inspector, all in the Chico District. Today she is on temporary duty at the General Office in San Jose working on special assignments for several Company officers. She also serves as an active member of the Internal Measures Team, a group that regularly collects customer feedback and measures customer satisfaction.

"Management support and encouragement has allowed it to happen," Mount said. *"I'm doing things I never thought I would be doing — public speaking, training, presentations, Continuous Improvement...all of which would have provoked fear and panic early*

on, but now are part of the job function I enjoy the most."

Additional thoughts from Vicky Mount...

On customer service: *"I remember one employee at a Customer Training Session who had been with Cal Water for 38 years saying he still recalls the day he started work when a supervisor told him, 'We are not in the business of selling water, we are in the business of customer service.'"*

On building relationships with customers, fellow employees and the Company itself: *"Sometimes we may catch ourselves concentrating on the negative part. But the focus always has to be on what is working and what is positive, and if it's not working, then be part of the solution. It's all about attitude and cooperation."*

On taking risks: *"I would encourage new employees not to be afraid to 'venture out.' Don't back away when someone is trying to 'stretch you' or encourage you to move on to another position. Take on the challenge... Go for it and have fun!"*

A Cal Water Family Heritage...

"My ties with the Company go back to the very beginning with my Uncle Primo (Villarruz) starting in the lab as a chemist during the late twenties; then, his son, Benny served also as a chemist in the lab beginning in the mid-1940s. I joined Cal Water in June of 1951. Now starting my 53rd year with the Company, I am called Mother Superior in the Engineering Department and am the Company's longest-tenured employee (so I'm told)."

Anita Paramo, engineering secretary 2004;
Employed since 1951

Chapter 48

Discovering Sgt. Dominguez
and the Company's roots...

The United States was only eight years old when the name
Dominguez became known on the land that Spanish explorer Juan
Cabrillo called the Bay of Many Smokes. Fifty-nine-year-old Sgt.
Juan Jose Dominguez had just retired from the Spanish army and was
awarded "grazing rights" to the first and largest of the Spanish land
grants in all of California. It was a favor bestowed upon him by a
friend, the Spanish governor of California, in recognition of
Dominguez's years of military service to the Spanish crown.
Dominguez named his retirement bonus, "Rancho San Pedro."

His grant included 75,000 acres in today's South Bay region of
Los Angeles County, where 11 present-day cities are located. Among
these are the communities of Carson, Hermosa Beach, Redondo
Beach, Torrance, Hawthorne and those on the Palos Verdes Peninsula,
all water utility service areas of California Water Service Company.

In November 1998, it was announced that the Dominguez Service Corporation — the parent of Dominguez Water Company, which
was formed to irrigate the original Spanish land grant — would merge
into the California Water Service Company. The purchase of the
Dominguez utility would round out Cal Water's association with the
colorful history of Rancho San Pedro. Explains Charles Porter, former
CEO and president of Dominguez Service Corp., *"With its acquisition
of Dominguez, Cal Water has found the root of all its South Bay
operations in the Greater Los Angeles area."* Within the Dominguez

service area is the site of the restored adobe home built in 1827 by Manuel Dominguez, a descendant of Sgt. Dominguez.

The merger of Cal Water with Dominguez was believed to be the largest merger of investor-owned water companies in California history and the largest single acquisition ever for Cal Water. The subsidiaries of Dominguez Service Corporation provided water service to a population of 140,000 in 20 communities throughout California. Its primary subsidiary was the Dominguez Water Company, with nearly 40,000 customers in and around the cities of Carson and Long Beach. One such customer was the Arco Refinery in the City of Carson, reportedly the fifth-largest refinery in the nation. Now owned by BP, the refinery is the largest customer served by Cal Water. The Dominguez water system had been formed as a mutual water company in 1911 to serve the Rancho's expanding agricultural operations. It had been designed by famed southern California engineer, William Mullholland, who later become head of the Los Angeles Department of Water and Power.

The other Dominguez subsidiaries included in the Cal Water merger were the Antelope Valley Water Company in northern Los Angeles County; Kern River Valley Water Company near Lake Isabella in Kern County; and a pending Dominguez acquisition of Redwood Valley Water Company in northern California. The merger was accomplished through a tax-free exchange of 1,778,000 shares of the California Water Service Group for all outstanding shares of Dominguez valued at approximately $47.6 million. The Group also assumed $10.5 million of outstanding net Dominguez debt.

With the Dominguez water utility system located adjacent to Cal Water's Hermosa-Redondo and Palos Verdes Peninsula Districts and the Hawthorne operations under lease, it was anticipated that the combined operations would bring long-term cost savings to Company customers. The Dominguez purchase would solidify Cal Water's position as the largest investor-owned water utility west of the Mississippi. It would be another two years, however, before the merger of the two companies was to receive final approval by the California Public Utilities Commission.

The land of Juan Jose Dominguez was once again the setting for a new business opportunity for the Group in June 1998, when the City of Manhattan Beach, adjacent to the Company's Hermosa-Redondo District, awarded CWS Utility Services a five-year contract to read the City's water meters on a bimonthly basis.

Earlier in the year, directors of the California Water Service Group announced the election of George A. Vera as the Board's newest member. He filled the vacancy created by the retirement of Edwin E. van Bronkhorst in December and was also elected a director of the Group's two wholly-owned subsidiaries, California Water Service Company and the CWS Utility Services. A Certified Public Accountant, Vera was director of finance and administration for the Packard Foundation, the nation's third-largest private foundation. He was a graduate of Harvard College and received his M.B.A. in finance and control from Harvard Business School.

Two additional Board actions were also taken during the year:

— A shareholders rights plan was adopted as a means to protect shareholder interests in the event of an attempted hostile acquisition of the Group. The plan was designed to maximize shareholder value by encouraging any prospective acquirer to negotiate with the Board.

— A resolution was adopted subject to shareholder approval to reincorporate the Group in the State of Delaware. Various advantages for the change were cited. Among these was the recognition that the state's legislature was responsive to business needs and acted quickly to adopt relevant new laws. In addition, it was felt that Delaware courts had developed an expertise in dealing with corporate issues, and that the State itself had created a sharper definition of board member responsibilities, enabling directors to act with greater certainty on issues affecting shareholders. The proposal would be adopted in April of 1999 following shareholder approval.

A Good Vehicle for Dominguez...

"Cal Water has exhibited an enduring ability to conduct good solid water operations and have good relations over the years with the PUC and be known for water service. Its solid reputation affords Dominguez a good vehicle in which to be a part."

Charles Porter, past president and CEO,
Dominguez Service Corp.

Chapter 49

"The right place, the right time, the right Company..."

T hose words written to shareholders in the spring of 2000 announced loudly and clearly that the Company was well-positioned and well-focused to *stay the course* as the industry's leader in traditional and innovative utility services.

The Group's enterprising new business efforts during the 20th Century's closing year were highlighted by the creation of a third subsidiary, the Washington Water Service Company. It marked the first acquisition by the California Water Service Group outside of California. With 14,000 customers, the new Company became the largest investor-owned water utility in the state of Washington. It was formed following the purchase of two Washington water utilities — Harbor Water Company in Gig Harbor and South Sound Utility Company in Olympia, which together were expected to increase annual Group revenue by $3.4 million.

Purchase of the new companies was in keeping with the Group's strategic goal of expanding operations beyond California through acquisitions, private-public partnerships and service agreements. Once again the transactions were completed through a tax-free exchange of stock, with 315,000 shares of Group stock issued in exchange for all shares of the two acquired companies. The total value of the purchase was $11.5 million, including the assumption of $3 million in debt. As has been the Group's policy in past acquisitions, all staff members of the acquired companies were offered the opportunity to remain as employees of Washington Water Service Company. Customer rates were not increased as a result of the merger.

As plans were being finalized for the Group's newest subsidiary serving the northwest, CWS Utility Services continued its own aggressive expansion program. Billing contracts were received from two southern California cities — Vista in northern San Diego County and El Segundo in Los Angeles County. Also finalized was the 15-year agreement for the operation and maintenance of the water system being created in the Rural North Vacaville Water District in Solano County. As previously noted, CWS Utility Services had been selected by the water district to design and construct an entirely new system in an unincorporated area of the county.

Capping its new business activities for the year, CWS Utility Services made an equity investment in QMS, a meter-reading company from Yorba Linda, California. The firm had been awarded a five-year meter-reading contract by the City of Santa Fe, New Mexico, thus providing Cal Water a presence in a third western state.

One of the most exciting developments among the many during 1999 involved the Group's regulated subsidiary, California Water Service Company. Cal Water was given governmental authority to build, own and operate a surface water treatment facility in Bakersfield, California, in a growing new area of the City. The Northeast Water Supply Project would eventually serve 15,000 new customers with a surface water supply being allocated by the City of Bakersfield from the community's Kern River. First phase of the project was scheduled for completion by 2002, producing 20 million gallons of water per day. Daily capacity at build-out was projected to reach 60 million gallons. Cal Water had been providing water utility service to Bakersfield, its largest District, since the Company's founding in 1926. The Bakersfield community had been cited as the eighth fastest-growing market in the United States.

One final new business activity during 1999 would again involve the Company's Bakersfield District, with the purchase of the Olcese Water District, adding 376 customers to the District's service area. The Olcese assets also included a surface water treatment plant and approximately 42,000 acre-feet of water deposited in the City of Bakersfield water bank. With the Olcese system becoming part of Cal Water's Bakersfield District for operational and rate-making purposes, it was anticipated that water rates for its customers would decrease.

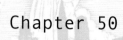

Chapter 50

The results are in...

Ｉt had been a dramatic and exciting five-year period for the Company as its accomplishments were tallied through Dec. 31, 2000. Clearly, those years represented one of the most remarkable periods for growth and change in Company history. The Foy/Nelson management team, which assumed command of California Water Service Group in early 1996, had held true to its vision and promise...*to create the team and build a Company dedicated to being **the** leader in providing communities and customers with traditional and innovative utility services.*

The results of their five-year stewardship told the story:
• Annual revenue increased $79 million to $244.8 million.
• Annual net income increased $5.2 million to $19.9 million.
• Number of communities served increased by 42 to 80.
• Population served increased by 500,000 to 2 million.

It indeed had been a rewarding time for the leadership and its team of dedicated employees.

The year 2000 had created its own excitement, highlighted by the formation of the Group's third subsidiary, the New Mexico Water Service Company, its first acquisition being the Rio Grande Utility Corporation, serving an unincorporated area 30 miles south of Albuquerque, New Mexico. The utility served 2,265 water and 1,600 waste-water customers in Valencia County. Purchase price was $2.3 million in cash with the assumption of $3.1 million of debt. Assets included water rights owned by the utility in addition to two waste-water treatment plants, the first such facilities owned by the California Water Service Group. The purchase was approved by the New Mexico Public Regulation Commission in the third quarter of 2001.

More activity during the year was also under way with the Group's Washington Water Service Company subsidiary. The Washington Utilities and Transportation Commission authorized the Company's purchase of two utilities in King and Pierce Counties, the largest of these being Mirromount Water Services in King County with 700 metered customers. In an effort to lower costs and develop an in-house engineering capacity, Washington Water also announced the purchase of Robischon Engineers, Inc.

Most of the Group's new business during 2000 would evolve around the activities of California Water Service Company. These included:

— Purchase of the Russell Valley Municipal Water District in Westlake, California. The acquisition of the government-owned system would help stabilize water rates in the Company's Westlake District.

— Final approval of the Dominguez Water Corporation merger which had come under a two-year review by the California Public Utilities Commission. Langdon W. Owen, a member of the Dominguez Corporation Board of Directors would be elected a director of the California Water Service Group at the Company's April 20, 2000, annual meeting. Sadly, he would only serve three years on the Board before his sudden death in the Spring of 2003.

The Company was about to enter its 75th year and a period that would bring unforeseen adversities, creating serious challenges to the Company and its new management team.

The restored adobe home of Manuel Dominguez, originally built in 1827, sits on the eastern slopes of Dominguez Hill within the Rancho Dominguez District service area of California Water Service Company. Manuel was a descendant of Sgt. Juan Jose Dominguez, who had been awarded grazing rights for the first and largest of the Spanish land grants located in the South Bay region of Los Angeles County.

Mayor Dee Hardison of Torrance, center, provided a helping hand to Terry Tamble, Cal Water's Rancho Dominguez district manager, during ribbon cutting ceremonies to observe opening of the Company's new customer service and operations center. Joining civic leaders and friends were Cal Water employees Don Jensen, Westlake district manager, fifth from right; John Foth, engineering manager, fourth from right; and Shannon Dean, director of corporate communications, third from right.

Chapter 51

Meeting the Challenge...

The year 2001 will long be remembered for the Twin Towers tragedy of September 11 and its rippling effect across the nation. Not since World War II had the Company implemented such stringent security measures throughout its systems as would be required following 9/11 to safeguard the water supply.

Compounding these difficulties during this 75th anniversary year were two additional factors that would seriously affect the bottom line.

Cool, wet weather throughout the Company's service areas significantly reduced customer water use and revenue. However, most ominous was the change in California's regulatory climate, which dramatically affected Company operations and the ongoing effort to maintain financial strength. Tragically, for almost a three-year period the California Public Utilities Commission would delay decisions in granting fair and timely rate increases to the Company and other water utilities seeking to offset rising costs. It gave a whole new meaning to the term "regulatory lag," an informal reference to delays in the rate-making processing. The situation was viewed as being the most severe in 30 years.

Most devastating was the inability to offset the cost of power which had risen 50 percent during the year and was the Company's second largest supply cost, totaling $20 million annually. Consequently, both earnings and operations were negatively affected requiring an austere Company-wide, cost-control program. Augmenting this effort was an intense program initiated by the Company's regulatory staff to file for multiple rate increases covering more than half of Company districts. At the same time, Company representatives joined forces with others in California's private water industry to initiate proactive efforts to ensure fair regulatory treatment in the future.

Revenue would remain relatively flat for the year as net income decreased 25 percent from Year 2000, lowering earnings by 34 cents per share.

While the difficulties of 2001 were being aggressively challenged, the year was not without important accomplishments and actions that would help grow and strengthen the Company.

Washington Water Service Company increased its customer base by 10 percent with the addition of 1,400 customers in three counties. To the south, Cal Water added 5,000 metered connections and infrastructure development to serve 120 new subdivisions.

Company-wide, more than 500 capital projects were completed during the year, including a new treatment plant in the Kern River Valley District. Also, construction began on Cal Water's $49-million Bakersfield Water Treatment plant, the largest capital project in Company history.

On the nonregulatory side, the Company signed five operating agreements in Washington state in 2001 and was selected to negotiate a 15-year lease agreement to operate the City of Commerce water system serving 1,085 customers adjacent to Cal Water's East Los Angeles operations.

Meanwhile, in northern California, San Jose Water Company signed an agreement with CWS Utilities Services for regular water testing of the San Jose utility's 220,000 customers. Cal Water's water quality laboratory was recognized within the industry as a top-rated facility, featuring highly technical and sophisticated equipment for bacteriological analyses and testing for organic and inorganic chemicals.

In March of 2001, the Board of Directors announced the election of water industry veteran Dan Stockton as vice president and chief information officer. He replaced retiring Ray Worrell, a 33-year veteran of Cal Water's information systems staff who had helped pioneer the Company's computerized billing program during the 1970s. With 29 years of executive experience in the water utility industry, Stockton brought a wealth of expertise in regulatory relations, marketing, finance and information systems. A past president of the California Water Association, he most recently had served as chief operating officer for Great Oaks Water Co. in San Jose.

Another outstanding business leader was elected a Company director in April of that year. Joining the Board was Douglas M. Brown, chairman of Talbot Financial Services of Albuquerque, New Mexico, a company he had co-founded in 1990 and under whose leadership had grown to $1.7 billion in annual sales. He was also president and CEO of Tuition Plan Consortium of Albuquerque, representing a group of more than 200 colleges and universities offering subscribers prepaid tuition plans at the participating schools. A Stanford University graduate, he followed in the footsteps of his late father, Robert Minge Brown, who for 40 years served with great distinction on the Cal Water Board, including 24 years as chairman.

Chapter 52

Staying the Course...

$\mathbf{F}$or a second consecutive year, Cal Water and other California water utilities were forced to cope with continuing delays in the state's rate-making process. And the financial community took notice. Wall Street made reference to the "dismal regulatory environment in California" as the California Public Utilities Commission again deferred action throughout 2002 in granting reasonable and timely rate increases. For the most part, these dealt with unavoidable expenses and capital improvements necessary to comply with increasing water quality standards and develop additional water supply while still meeting the rising cost of power.

Fortunately, weather conditions for 2002 had returned to normal in California, increasing customer water use and helping support the year's financial results. But management was fully aware that if regulatory difficulties were to persist into a third year, a sustained company-wide effort would be necessary to stay focused on the devised strategy to:

- counteract unfair delays in regulatory decisions,
- remain diligent in efforts to reduce expenses and increase efficiency and
- aggressively grow the Company in new and existing service areas.

A significant accomplishment in the regulatory area took place in October 2002 when Assembly Bill 2838 became California law. It was designed to ensure that regulated water utilities would be given timely rate relief by the State's Public Utilities Commission. The Company's regulatory staff, headed by Vice President Stan Ferraro, had joined forces with member companies of the California Water Association to spearhead the effort to gain passage of the bill authored by Assemblyman Joe Canciamilla. It was an encouraging sign that timely rate-making procedures might once again be back on track.

Efforts to grow the Company during the year added 8,600 customers, with nearly half coming from the Group's New Mexico Water Service Company, which had now completed purchase of the Rio Grande Corporation service area. The New Mexico subsidiary also announced during the year that an agreement had been signed to acquire National Utility Corporation with 1,600 customer services.

Existing service areas in California accounted for 3,900 of the new services added during 2002, while Washington Water Service Company recorded 600 new hookups.

The prospect of the Group's fifth subsidiary — the Hawaii Water Service Company — came on the horizon in 2002, when an agreement was signed to purchase the Kaanapali Water Corporation on the Island of Maui. Approval of the acquisition by the Hawaii regulatory agency was received in April 2003 at a purchase price of $8 million.

Earlier in the year, a valued friend and counselor to the Company, Dr. Robert K. Jaedicke, announced his resignation from the Board of Directors. He had served the Company with great distinction for 28 years under five chief executive officers. The author of numerous books and articles, Dr. Jaedicke was Professor Emeritus of Accounting and former Dean of the Stanford Graduate School of Business.

As 2002 came to a close, employees at the General Office in San Jose received word that the Company's long-time building superintendent, Raymond Woods, had died suddenly. Candida Rocha, a 25-year

Cal Water employee at the San Jose headquarters, probably best expressed the mood that prevailed:

"The pews were filled when I arrived for Ray's services at his church in Milpitas. It seemed like our entire General Office staff was there to honor Ray, a man of honesty and great integrity. Even retirees came. To me that packed church said a lot about our Company. No one had said they were too busy. It said our people care enough to take time to honor one of our own and pay tribute to a man of character."

Chapter 53

Finally! The logjam is broken...

The first quarter of 2003 began on a depressing note as the largest rate case in Company history remained stalled within the State's regulatory process. The lag had now extended into its 22nd month with no decision in sight. Furthering the Company's plight was the reduction in water sales brought on by unseasonable spring weather resulting in the coldest, wettest April on record. When the financial results were announced for the first three months, earnings had dropped five cents per share. But despite the bleak beginning, amazingly, 2003 would become a turnaround year for the Company, with revenue for the entire year reaching an all-time high of $277 million.

The regulatory logjam had begun to disintegrate in the spring of that year. The Public Utilities Commission announced in May it was granting recovery of $5.4 million in lost revenue, which the Company incurred 2 1/2 years earlier when the cost of electrical power had skyrocketed. The remaining months of 2003 would bring approval for other long-pending rate cases, resulting in the prospect for new annual revenue of $26 million and the release of another $9 million in surcharges that the Company had collected and was required to hold over for the past 24 months. But the biggest effect was shown in 2003's fourth-quarter financial results — net income rose 146 percent and earnings per share were up 116 percent over the prior year.

Unfortunately, the regulatory delays suffered by the Company since 2001 would eventually be recognized by the financial community. Both *Moody's* and *Standard and Poor's* financial services would announce that they would be lowering the credit rating on senior secured debt for the Group's California Water Service Company subsidiary due to the unfavorable regulatory environment in California. For a number of years, Cal Water was one of two water companies within the United States that had held the highest credit rating among all private water utilities. Company officials expressed confidence they would regain that position once the full effect of the regulatory turnaround was felt. But for the most part, 2003 was an upbeat year, bringing further news that would complement the prevailing excitement created by the improved financial picture.

Hawaii Water Service Company officially became a subsidiary in April 2003 with formal acquisition of the Kaanapali Water Corporation. The system contributed 500 customers to the Group's two-percent growth for the year and brought a highly skilled, experienced staff of water utility professionals into the fold, headed by Kaanapali's General Manager Jeffrey K. Eng. Within the service area are ten large resorts and eight condominium projects requiring water service to several thousand residents and guests.

Two years under construction, Cal Water's $49-million state-of-the-art water treatment plant in the Bakersfield District officially opened in June of 2003 — on time and on budget. It was the largest capital project in Company history and would become an integral part of Bakersfield operations, meeting the water quality and supply needs of 95,000 customers. The new plant would allow the City of Bakersfield to increase population in the city's dynamic growth area to the Northeast. Even if it were to operate at only 1/3 of its capacity, the new plant could provide a glass of water everyday to each person in North America.

In late summer, the Company raised $43.8 million in capital through a public offering of 1.75 million in new shares of common stock to pay off debt and strengthen the balance sheet. Percentage of equity to total capitalization increased from 44 percent to 47 percent. The Company also completed a debt financing program during the year that provided annual savings of $2 million in interest expense.

Key leadership appointments were announced during the year, starting in March with Richard D. Nye being named vice president, chief financial officer and treasurer of the Group, succeeding Gerald F. Feeney, who was retiring after nearly 27 years of service. Nye, a Certified Public Accountant, had served most recently as vice president and acting chief financial officer at Cornerstone Propane Partners, LP. Previously he had held management positions at Halliburton Company and Frito-Lay. Feeney began his Cal Water career in 1976 as controller and advanced to vice president, CFO and treasurer in 1995. He was truly a dedicated and unique employee, not only excelling as the Company's top financial officer, but also as one who had developed lasting, personal relationships with co-workers. At many retirement dinners, he was called upon to serve as master of ceremonies — a testament to his years of genuine concern for the well-being and success of his fellow employees.

Also announced were two managerial appointments. Paul D. Risso, who had served as district manager in both Cal Water's Stockton and Visalia Districts, was named general manager of New Mexico Water Service Company, and William L. Koehler was hired to manage the Company's Redwood Valley District in northern California.

Finally, in April 2003, two distinguished professionals in their respective fields joined the Company's Board of Directors. Elected were Bonnie G. Hill, head of the consulting firm of B. Hill Enterprises, LLC, and David N. Kennedy, former Director of the California Department of Water Resources.

Hill, whose firm specialized in corporate governance and organizational and public policy issues, also was COO for Icon Blue, a Los Angeles-based marketing firm. She had previously served as Senior Vice President, Community Relations, for *The Los Angeles Times*, and President and CEO of *The Times Mirror Foundation*.

Kennedy, a widely respected expert on California water issues, had served as Assistant General Manager of the Metropolitan Water District of Southern California before his appointment to the state's Water Resources post during Gov. George Deukmejian's administration.

The Group's 2004 Board of Directors, seated, left to right, Peter C. Nelson, President and Chief Executive Officer, and Robert W. Foy, Chairman of the Board; standing, left to right, Bonnie G. Hill, President of B. Hill Enterprises, L.L.C., Chief Operating Officer of Icon Blue; Richard P. Magnuson, Private Venture Capital Investor; David N. Kennedy, former Director, California Department of Water Resources; Edward D. Harris, Jr., M.D., Professor Emeritus, Stanford University Medical Center; Linda R. Meier, a Director of Greater Bay Bancorp, the Peninsula Community Foundation and National Advisory Board of the Haas Public Service Center; George A. Vera, Vice President and Chief Financial Officer, the David & Lucile Packard Foundation; Douglas M. Brown, President and Chief Executive Officer of Tuition Plan Consortium.

Districts and Managers — 2004

California Water Service	Customers	Manager
Antelope Valley (Incl. Fremont Valley, Lake Hughes, Lancaster and Leona Valley)	1,300	Tim Treloar, Dist. Manager
Bakersfield	60,900	Tim Treloar, Dist. Manager
		Bill Harper, Asst. Dist. Manager
		Rudy Valles, Jr., Asst. Dist. Manager
Bayshore (Incl. San Mateo, San Carlos, South San Francisco, Colma and Broadmoor)	52,700	Tyrone Robinson, Dist. Manager
		Paul Baker, Asst. Dist. Manager
Bear Gulch (Incl. Atherton, Woodside, Portola Valley and portions of Menlo Park)	17,600	Darin Duncan, Dist. Manager
Chico (Incl. Hamilton City)	25,200	Mark Lightcap, Dist. Manager
Dixon	2,900	Frank Volpi, Local Manager
East Los Angeles (Incl. City of Commerce)	27,600	David Karraker, Dist. Manager
Kern River Valley (Incl. Bodfish, Kernville, Lakeland, South Lake, Mtn. Shadows and Wofford Heights)	4,200	Chris Whitley, Local Manager
King City	2,300	Terry Hughes, Local Manager
Livermore	17,600	John Freeman, Local Manager
Los Altos (Incl. portions of Cupertino, Los Altos Hills, Mt. View and Sunnyvale)	18,400	Ron Richardson, Dist. Manager
Marysville	3,800	Lee Seidel, Dist. Manager
Oroville	3,500	Gary Alt, Dist. Manager
Rancho Dominguez (Incl. Carson, Palos Verdes Estates, Rancho Palos Verdes, Rolling Hills, Rolling Hills Estates, Hermosa Beach, Redondo Beach, Hawthorne and portions of Long Beach, Compton, Harbor City, Los Angeles, Torrance)	89,300	Terry Tamble, Dist. Manager
		Ross Moilan, Asst. Dist. Manager
Redwood Valley (Incl. Lucerne, Duncans Mills, Guerneville, Dillon Beach and portions of Santa Rosa)	1,900	Bill Koehler, Dist. Manager
Salinas	27,700	James Smith, Dist. Manager
Selma	5,600	James Smith, Dist. Manager
Stockton	42,000	Henry Wind, Dist. Manager
Visalia	33,300	Phil Mirwald, Dist. Manager
Westlake (Incl. portion of Thousand Oaks)	7,000	Don Jensen, Dist. Manager
Willows	2,300	Rob Thompson, Local Manager
Cal Water Subtotal	**447,100**	
Hawaii Water Service Co.	500	Jeffrey K. Eng, Gen. Manager
New Mexico Water Service Co.	4,100	Paul Risso, Gen. Manager
Washington Water Service Co.	14,700	Michael P. Ireland, President
Total Customers	**466,400**	

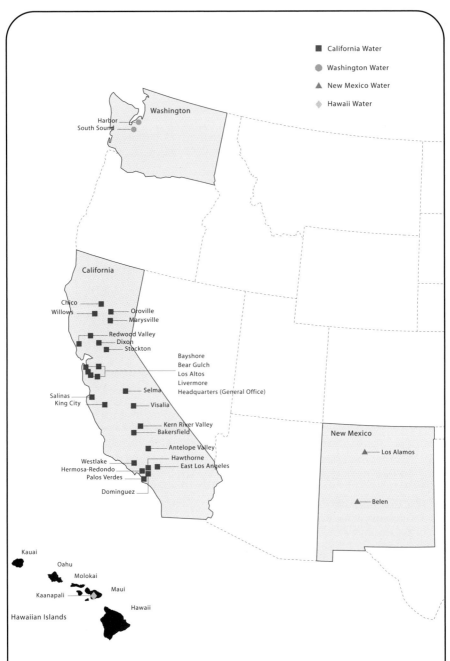

California Water
Washington Water
New Mexico Water
Hawaii Water

Washington

Harbor
South Sound

California

Chico
Willows
Oroville
Marysville
Redwood Valley
Dixon
Stockton
Bayshore
Bear Gulch
Los Altos
Livermore
Headquarters (General Office)
Salinas
King City
Selma
Visalia
Kern River Valley
Bakersfield
Antelope Valley
Westlake
Hawthorne
Hermosa-Redondo
East Los Angeles
Palos Verdes
Dominguez

New Mexico

Los Alamos

Belen

Kauai
Oahu
Molokai
Kaanapali
Maui
Hawaii
Hawaiian Islands

Through its five subsidiaries operating in California, Hawaii, New Mexico and Washington, the California Water Service Group provides water utility service to more than 100 communities with a combined population of two million.

226

Chapter 54

Going the Extra Mile...

A s CEO, Pete Nelson would announce to stockholders at the annual meeting in April of 2004, the dramatic financial turnaround during the prior year came only through the dedicated teamwork and cooperative spirit of the Company's 813 employees. *"It was a perfect example,"* Nelson explained, *"of people going the extra mile to overcome adversity during a very difficult period for the Company. We are proud and grateful for their service."*

Clearly, Nelson's report to stockholders at the annual meeting was upbeat in support and praise of the Company's employees and the vital role they played in tackling the difficulties of the past three years.

The 2003 annual report highlighted specific examples of employees throughout the Company going above and beyond to provide excellent customer service. *"You can build the best treatment plant in the world,"* Nelson said, *"but it still takes people to provide the service. That's where we really have the advantage — with the people that work here."*

Nelson told stockholders that despite the regulatory difficulties of the recent past, customer service excelled to an all-time high as indicated in Company "satisfaction" surveys. When customers were asked to rate the Company on service, 92 percent rated their service "excellent" or "very good," up from 85 percent four years earlier. Moreover, he said, the survey indicated that 19 of every 20 customers had their inquiries answered on the very first call to a Company representative, a 12-percent improvement over "first call" results shown in past surveys.

With regard to training, Nelson told stockholders that even with the increased emphasis on efficient operations during 2003, the Company was able to provide 12,000 hours of training to employees, and more than 500 employees achieved higher levels of certification from the State of California either in water distribution or water treatment.

In his comments at the annual meeting, Chairman Bob Foy made special reference to the work and stature of the Company's directors, whom he termed *"an extremely talented group of professionals, all leaders in their respective fields. Our Board members,"* Foy said, *"each brought a unique expertise and experience to the table, with specialties ranging from finance to corporate governance, from accounting to water supply."* He made specific reference to the work of the Board's Corporate Governance program headed by Director Richard P. Magnuson. At a time when the nation's investors had become increasingly concerned about corporate conduct, Foy said it was both an honor and pleasure to serve on the Board of the California Water Service Group, which he emphasized has always been committed to conducting its business with openness and with utmost integrity.

The adverse regulatory conditions of the past three years did not affect the Company's long-standing commitment to stockholders regarding the payment of quarterly dividends. The Board had announced in January of 2004 that the annual dividend was being raised for the 37th consecutive year (to $1.13 per share), and would be paid to common stock shareholders for the 59th consecutive year.

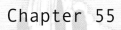

Chapter 55

Building the legacy...

T he Company's 1996 annual report predicted that the year would be remembered as a landmark for California Water Service Company. Eight years down the road, that forecast was *right on*!

When Bob Foy and Peter Nelson completed that first year as Cal Water's new management team, they announced that a new vision had been created for the Company — one that required change. They recognized the underlying potential for the Company, but also realized they were facing a competitive environment never before experienced in the private water utility industry. Their expectations and vision for the future would inspire the staff of Cal Water to embrace the change and meet the challenge.

The new leadership had been entrusted with a great Company...one that had created a legacy of service and a sterling reputation for integrity, professionalism and financial stability.

When Christopher Chenery formed the Company in 1926, his team from the Fresno acquisition — Jackson, Camy, Hulick, Barnum, Shupe, Walthall, Harris and Suters — was an incredible find. They were men of substance, whose exceptional talent and integrity helped create the foundation of professionalism for which Cal Water is known today. Their impact on the Company would be felt throughout the years.

In his time, Ralph Elsman was the driving force behind the Company's emphasis on quality and service. Such was the view held by Harry Kerr, former vice president for public affairs who had known Elsman since 1952. According to Kerr, the effects of Elsman's demand for quality and excellence would pervade the Company's culture through to the present day. As Elsman's 1920 interview in *Forbes* magazine had so indicated, his stated philosophy for "doing the right thing" would help build the Company's reputation after he had taken command in 1939.

"There is only one way to get public opinion on your side in the public utility business," he had said, *"that is by being fair and square and honest with yourself, with your employees and with the public whom you serve."* Elsman encouraged his employees never to forget the importance of maintaining customer service, saying the paramount rule in the public utility business was that *"dependable service to the consumer always came first."* Jack Call, who served as Cal Water's corporate secretary in the fifties, remarked: *"Elsman was very much the man on the job when it came to satisfying the customer."*

"The customer service ethic," explains Paul Risso, general manager of the New Mexico Water Service Company, *"has been at the top of the Company's priorities ever since my first day at work. It is something that has been passed on from person to person and is ingrained in our daily work habits. I noticed it especially out in the field when I first started with the Company during the seventies. It was something that was always really emphasized. I can remember the construction superintendent in Stockton, Frank Simonds, giving us advice on how to treat the customer and how to face a difficult situation. 'Always remember,' he said, 'when dealing with the customer, our name is California Water SERVICE Company!' I've never forgotten it."*

"Service has always been a hallmark of the Company," explains Chairman Bob Foy, *"and is part of the name for each of our subsid-*

iaries. When someone is first hired, we start talking about customer service, whether it be a utility worker or a new engineer or someone in the accounting department. Customer service is something that is ingrained in all Cal Water people. It comes with being a Cal Water professional."

According to Jeptha Wade, Jr., Cal Water's retired chief engineer, professionalism in the water business, to a great extent, can be broadcast through the way facilities are maintained. *"We have been entrusted with operating water systems in our communities that represent an investment of many millions of dollars,"* Wade said, *"but the only parts that can be seen by the community are a few pump stations and couple of storage tanks. To a great extent the whole impression of the Company may be colored by what facilities actually can be seen. Because we are dealing with a product that is such an important part of the public health, our facilities must have a clean and attractive appearance and look like we are meant to do business. Fred Dodge was very much that way. I got it from him, and that philosophy has prevailed throughout our Company. If we show the public that the outside of the facilities look great, then those things underground...the wells and the pipes must also be in pretty good shape."*

The reputation of Cal Water has also resulted from the creativity and innovations initiated by Company employees in water quality, engineering, information systems, and all other Company disciplines that have been so vital to the Company's well-being and success over 78 years of operation. Further strengthening Cal Water's professional stature has been its consistent leadership role in support of programs to benefit the water utility industry. This has included active participation in the professional programs of the American Water Works Association and numerous other water groups working at local, state and national levels in support of water issues and programs. Former

President and CEO Don Houck served two terms as president of the California Water Association as did Vice President Dan Stockton, the Company's present-day head of Information Systems. On the national scene, former chairman and CEO Ralph Lindberg gained an industry-wide reputation during the eighties for his work as president of the National Association of Water Companies, a post which CEO Pete Nelson is scheduled to assume in the fall of 2006.

But Nelson has emphasized that while it is important for the Group to build its professional reputation within the water industry, the focus must always be on serving the Company's three constituencies — customers, employees and stockholders. *"Good decisions,"* he said, *"always balance the needs of these three important groups."*

Regarding the Company's performance on behalf of stockholders, the record speaks for itself: since first becoming a public company in 1945, Cal Water has never missed a year paying its stated dividend. Further, when the Company announced a dividend increase in January 2004, it marked the 37th consecutive year the dividend has been raised. According to Robert Clark, associate vice president of Dean Witter Investments, who has followed Cal Water stock for 40 years:

"I have attended close to 30 annual meetings over the years and have never been disappointed by Cal Water. The beauty has been there have been no surprises. Cal Water has been a wonderful investment for my customers. It gives them security and peace of mind."

Finally, no discussion on the historical accomplishments and professionalism of California Water Service Company would be complete without a "tip of the hat" to a courageous past.

Throughout the years, courage has taken many forms in building Cal Water's heritage...including that such as demonstrated by Storekeeper Carl Stahlecker in 1941. He had placed his job on the line when he agreed to lead Bakersfield employees in their effort to unionize the District to bring change when change was needed. It was also shown by an unwavering Ralph Elsman, who had pledged his personal assets as collateral to literally save the Company in 1945, thus enabling its public stock offering to move forward. And then there has been the courage of Cal Water directors whose Board decisions have not wavered when difficult choices had to be made over the years to best serve the Company. There have been countless other examples of brave actions among those in the Cal Water family, mostly unsung, but nonetheless important in contributing to the Company's legacy.

"When I came to the Company in 1996," explains CEO Peter Nelson, *"I was struck by the talent and commitment of 650 men and women who at that time were part of the Cal Water team. Our customers and communities were being well-served by very skilled people, supported by a wide range and depth of talent at our Company headquarters. Today in 2004, we have over 816 employees serving a population of two million in four western states. Our Company has enjoyed great success through 78 magnificent years. In the final analysis, it has been the dedication and spirit of our employees who have enthusiastically embraced our culture for the benefit of our customers and shareholders. What a privilege it is to be a part of that team."*

Introducing. . .

California Water Service Group 2004

Antelope Valley

Bakersfield

Bayshore

Bear Gulch

Chico

Dixon

East Los Angeles

General Office - Executive Building

General Office - Accounting

General Office - Engineering

General Office - Information Systems

General Office - Water Quality

General Office - Human Resources, Purchasing, Rates, Stores

General Office - Various Departments

Hawaii Water Service

Kern River Valley

Livermore

Los Altos

Marysville

New Mexico Water Service

Oroville

Rancho Dominguez

Redwood Valley - Lucerne

Redwood Valley - Guerneville

Salinas/King City

Selma

Stockton

Visalia

Washington Water Service

Westlake

Willows

Council Presidents
California Water Service Company
Utility Workers Union of America — AFL-CIO

Carl Stahlecker	T. C. Dennis
Elmer Neubert	Ken Huber
Mervyn Heatlie	Mike Jones
Richard Trueblood	Gene Darter
Albert Jacobson	Toni Ruggle
Dave Diamond	Arlene Dallman
Mick Palmer	Ida Huber
Harry Miller	Marty Garton

Presidents
California Water Service Company
International Federation of Professional
and Technical Engineers — AFL-CIO
(Chartered Feb. 7, 1968)

Dick Menden

Carey E. Neal, Jr.

Mike Fogel

Ed Harr

Keith Van der Maaten

Fred Rios

Bibliography/Source Material

—<u>America in the Forties</u> — A Reader's Digest Book, Published 1998 — The Reader's Digest Assn. Inc., Harold Rabinowitz, Editor in Chief

—<u>Boston Properties Center News</u> — March/April 2000, The "Old Fed" Reserve Bank Bldg., San Francisco

—<u>Business Journal</u> — San Jose, California, Sept. 23, 1996

—California Water Service Company and Group Annual Reports — 1927 through 2003

—California Water Service Company Corporate and District Histories as filed with California Public Utilities Commission

—California Water Service Company and Group Engineering/Water Quality Facilities Brochure and miscellaneous Company brochures

—California Water Service Company, "Leaks and Drips" — Employee Publication
    1943 — June, July, October, November,
    1944 — January, April, May, June, July, August, September, October, November, December
    1945 — January, February, March, May, June, July, November, December
    1946 — January, April, May/June, July, October, November, December
    1947 — January, February

—California Water Service Company, minutes of meetings — Board of Directors
    Dec. 21, 1926, Dec. 23, 1926, Dec. 30, 1926, Dec. 31, 1926, Feb. 1, 1927, Feb. 10, 1927, Feb. 28, 1927, April 15, 1927, April 19, 1927, April 21, 1927, April 22, 1927, April 28, 1927, May 31, 1927, July 29, 1927, Dec. 30, 1927, Jan. 30, 1928, Dec. 12, 1928, July 23, 1928, April 11, 1945

—California Water Service Company and Group, News Releases, various release dates

—California Water Service Company and Group, <u>Pipeline</u> — Internal Newsletters:
    All Issues: 1982-2004

—California Water Service Company and Group, <u>The Well</u> — Internal Newsletters
    All Issues: 1996-2004

—<u>Chicago Tribune</u>, July 2, 2000

—Correspondence, telegrams, memos: Robert Minge Brown, Christopher T. Chenery, Fred L. Dodge, Earl C. Elliott, Sr., Frank F. Walker, Ralph D. Lindberg

—<u>Dynasty of Water-The Story of the American Water Works Company</u> by Gilbert Cross
    Published 1991 — American Water Works Company, Inc.

—Filings and Decisions, California Public Utilities Commission: Decision No. 41092, January 6, 1948

—<u>Forbes</u>, May 29, 1920

—<u>Fresno Republican</u>, Jan. 8, 1930

—McCutchen, Doyle, Brown & Enersen — San Francisco Firm History, California Water Service Company Files

—New York Times, Dec. 4, 1937, Jan. 5, 1973, Jan. 18, 1964

—Railroad Commission of State of California, Oct. 16, 1926, Decision No. 17481;
  Feb. 2, 1927, Decision No.17949; March 2, 1927, Decision No. 18037; March 21, 1927,
  Decision No. 18084; March 24, 1927, Decision No. 18102; March 24, 1927, Decision No. 18101;
  March 28, 1927, Decision No. 18111; Dec. 23, 1927, Decision No. 19161; March 12, 1928,
  Decision No. 19467; March 31, 1928, Decision No. 19540; May 29, 1928, Decision No. 19837;
  Nov. 16, 1928, Decision No. 20493

—Reflections on Water — A Centennial History of Philadelphia Suburban Water Co.—1886-1986
  Edited and Compiled by Jerry A. Sacchetti

—R.L. Polk's Fresno County Directory, 1927

—San Francisco Chronicle, Nov. 30, 1994, Obituary, Robert Minge Brown

—San Joaquin Light and Power Company Annual Reports — 1925-26

—San Jose Mercury News, Oct. 8, 1940 — Headquarters to San Jose, Dec. 20, 1956 — Officers
  named; Dec. 16, 1965 — Officers named

—Secretariat by Raymond G. Woolfe, Jr., Published 1974 and 1981

—Southern California Water Co. by Robert R. Morris, A History — 1929-1999; published 1999

—The California Water Atlas, published 1978-79, The State of California, prepared by the Governor's
  Office of Planning & Research in cooperation with the California Department of Water
  Resources, Project Director and Editor: William L. Kahrl

—The Fabulous Century—1920-1930, Published 1969 by Time Life Books

—The Magazine of Western Finance, September 1928

—Utility Spotlight—A Weekly Executive Service of Corporate Intelligence, Inc., Dec. 27, 1956

—Who's Who in America 1930-1931

Interviews:

(All interviews conducted by Kenneth J. Roed on dates or during periods indicated)

*Louise Alba, Jan. 21, 2000; office staff, East Los Angeles District, California Water Service
  Company, retired

Eva Borak, Aug. 27, 1999; personal law secretary for 46 years to Robert Minge Brown, McCutchen,
  Doyle, Brown & Enersen law firm, San Francisco, retired

*Robert Minge Brown, past chairman and chief executive, California Water Service Company;
  informal meetings with author 1989 through 1993 reviewing Company historical events

Ray Castro, Jan. 21, 2000; district manager, Selma District, California Water Service Company, retired

Dino Coppe, Oct. 21, 1999; manager of field operations and construction, California Water Service
  Company, retired

Mike Camy, Oct. 18, 1999; district manager, Stockton District, California Water Service Company, retired

Robert J. Clark, Aug. 26, 1999; associate vice president, Morgan Stanley, San Jose, CA

*Rito Castanon, Sept. 21, 1999; inspector, Stockton District, California Water Service Company, retired

*Jack Call, July 15, 1999; corporate secretary, California Water Service Company, retired

Walt Delsigne, Jan. 22, 2000; district manager, Hermosa-Redondo District, California Water Service Company, retired

Dave Diamond, Jan. 21, 2000; district manager, East Los Angeles District, California Water Service Company, retired

S.M. DiMartino, Sept. 21, 1999; manager, data processing, California Water Service Company, retired

*Fred L. Dodge, past president, California Water Service Company; informal meetings with author reviewing Company historical events, 1988-1990

Audrey Dodge, Sept. 20, 1999; widow of Fred Dodge, former president, California Water Service Company

Ken Dow, Sept. 23, 1999; district manager, Visalia District, California Water Service Company, retired

*Richard Eilert, Oct. 18, 1999; auditor, California Water Service Company, retired

Paul G. Ekstrom, October, 1999; vice president, customer service, corporate secretary, California Water Service Company

*Nancy (Elsman) Pierce, July 27, 1999; daughter of Ralph Elsman, former president, California Water Service Company

Francis "Stan" Ferraro, Jan. 24, 2000; vice president, regulatory matters, California Water Service Company

Gerry F. Feeney, Oct. 21, 1999; vice president, chief financial officer, California Water Service Company, retired

Robert W. Foy, Nov. 16, 1999; chairman of the Board, California Water Service Company

Robert R. Guzzetta, Jan. 28, 2000; vice president, engineering and water quality, California Water Service Company

Eugene Grant, April 23, 1999; district manager, Chico District, California Water Service Company, retired

Elizabeth Grant, April 23, 1999; granddaughter of Earl C. Elliot, past president, California Water Service Company

Donald L. Houck, Oct. 19, 1999; past president, California Water Service Company, retired

*Harry T. Kerr, March 18, 1999; past vice president, California Water Service Company, retired

*C. A. (Al) Larson, Jr., July 14,1999; past corporate secretary, California Water Service Company, retired

Bob D. Lewis, Sept. 23, 1999; district manager, Bakersfield District, California Water Service Company, retired

Mary Lindberg, Sept. 20, 1999; widow of Ralph D. Lindberg, past chairman and chief executive officer, California Water Service Company

Robert Momand, Oct. 21, 1999; draftsman, California Water Service Company, retired

Gene Myers, April 15, 2004; storekeeper, Rancho Dominguez, California Water Service Company

Ambassador L. W. Lane, Jr., Nov. 16, 1999; Board of Directors, California Water Service Company, retired

Vicky Mount, April 15, 2004; customer serviceline program coordinator, California Water Service Company

Christine McFarlane, Oct. 21, 1999; vice president, human resources, California Water Service Company

Phyllis (Massey) Lovoi, April 20, 1999; executive secretary, California Water Service Company, retired

*William Nahmens, July 16, 1999; district manager, Bear Gulch District, California Water Service Company, retired

Peter C. Nelson, Sept. 23,1996; president and chief executive officer, California Water Service Company; interviewed by Danna Bergstrom, The Business Journal, San Jose, CA; phone interview by Ken Roed, May 11, 2004

Roberta H. Nelson, June 19, 2000; assistant secretary, California Water Service Company, retired

Anita Paramo, July 14, 1999; secretary, engineering, California Water Service Company

Velma Potter, April 20, 1999; executive secretary, California Water Service Company, retired

Charles Porter, Jan. 22, 2000; president and chief executive officer, Dominguez Water Corporation, retired

Paul Risso, Jan. 21, 2000; general manager, New Mexico Water Service Company

Parker Robinson, Aug. 26 and Oct. 19, 1999; assistant chief engineer, California Water Service Company, retired

Candida Rocha, April 14, 2004; water conservation coordinator, California Water Service Company

Ralph Steiber, Aug. 25, 1999; assistant chief engineer, California Water Service Company, retired

John Simpson, October, 1999; assistant secretary and manager of new business, California Water Service Company

C. H. "Bud" Stump, April 15-16, 1999; chairman and chief executive officer, California Water Service Company, retired

Vertalyne Stolp, Sept. 21, 1999; widow of A.L. (LaDreu) Stolp, manager of San Mateo District, California Water Service Company

Albert Stregger, Aug. 25, 1999; district manager, Bear Gulch District, California Water Service Company, retired

Dorothy Shepard, Aug. 20, 1999; payroll supervisor, California Water Service Company, retired

Raymond H. Taylor, Jan. 24, 2000; vice president, operations, California Water Service Company

Gila Torres, Aug. 25, 1999; executive secretary, California Water Service Company, retired

Sue Robinson, Oct. 21, 1999; daughter of Joseph Viguier, former vice president and general manager, California Water Service Company

Ben Villarruz, Aug. 24, 1999; laboratory assistant, California Water Service Company, retired

*Ida White, Oct. 21, 1999; former executive secretary, California Water Service Company, retired

Raymond L. Worrell, Aug. 15, 1999; vice president/chief information officer, California Water Service Company, retired

Jeptha A. Wade, Jr., March 17, 1999; April 21,1999; April 5, 2000; vice president and chief engineer, California Water Service Company, retired

* Deceased

Photography

Christopher T. Chenery, courtesy of Raymond Woolfe, Jr., author of book, Secretariat

San Jose Water Company Headquarters Building, courtesy of San Jose Water Company

San Francisco Federal Reserve Bldg. ("The Old Fed"), courtesy of the Boston Properties, Inc.

San Joaquin Light and Power Building, Fresno, California (circa 1926), courtesy of the collections of the Fresno County Library

Fred Rios, General Office Photography, California Water Service Company

Photographs — Courtesy of Dorothy Shepard, Phyllis Lovoi, Walt Delsigne, S. M. DiMartino, Bobbi Nelson, Jeptha A. Wade, Jr., Ben Villarruz, Vertalyne Stolp, C. H. Stump, Ralph Steiber, Parker Robinson, Paul Risso, Velma Potter, Charles Porter, William Nahmens, Ambassador L. W. Lane, Jr., Robert Momand, Mary Lindberg, Annette White, Bob D. Lewis, C. A. (Al) Larson, Jr., Elizabeth Grant, Robert W. Foy, Nancy Elsman Pierce, Ken Dow, Dave Diamond, Audrey Dodge, Jack Call, Rito Castanon, Mike Camy, Mrs. Lee Johnson, Dick Balocco, Bob Day

Index

252